W9-AUK-584

IT HAPPENED IN ALASKA

It Happened In Series

IT HAPPENED IN
ALASKA

Diane Olthuis

TWODOT®

GUILFORD, CONNECTICUT
HELENA, MONTANA
AN IMPRINT OF THE GLOBE PEQUOT PRESS

To buy books in quantity for corporate use
or incentives, call **(800) 962–0973**
or e-mail **premiums@GlobePequot.com**.

A · TWODOT® · BOOK

Copyright © 2006 by Morris Book Publishing, LLC

All rights reserved. No part of this book may be reproduced or transmitted in any form by any means, electronic or mechanical, including photocopying and recording, or by any information storage and retrieval system, except as may be expressly permitted by the 1976 Copyright Act or by the publisher. Requests for permission should be made in writing to The Globe Pequot Press, P.O. Box 480, Guilford, Connecticut 06437.

TwoDot is a registered trademark of Morris Book Publishing, LLC.

Text design by Nancy Freeborn
Map by M. A. Dubé © Morris Book Publishing, LLC

Front cover photo: Horses pulling sleds on the Valdez Trail, Library of Congress Prints & Photographs Division, LC-USZ62-123547
Back cover photo: Traveling with reindeer, Library of Congress Prints & Photographs Division

Library of Congress Cataloging-in-Publication Data
Olthuis, Diane, 1951–
  It happened in Alaska / Diane Olthuis.—1st ed.
    p. cm.—(It happened in series)
  Includes bibliographical references and index.
  ISBN-13: 978-0-7627-3908-0
  ISBN-10: 0-7627-3908-8
  1. Alaska—History—Anecdotes. I. Title. II. Series.
  F904.6.O48 2006
  979.8—dc22

                                                            2005035143

Manufactured in the United States of America
First Edition/Third Printing

To Jon Gantenbein and Stephen Finger

CONTENTS

CONTENTS

ACKNOWLEDGMENTS

Before the usual opening hour, I unlocked the Hope and Sunrise Historical and Mining Museum for author Cherry Jones. While I aided her in researching her book about Alaskan women, she encouraged me to write a book about the events that had shaped Alaska. The project sounded exciting, so I contacted Stephanie Hester of The Globe Pequot Press. Under Stephanie's patient guidance, this book took shape.

I've traveled to most of the chapter locations, but needed to verify the story facts, and to that end I rushed into the Hope and Sunrise Community Library, where Sue Anderson, Gail Dalrymple, Beth Kaser, and Fayrene Sherritt generously assisted me in finding books on each topic. I found additional books on the shelf behind Ann Miller's desk at the Hope and Sunrise Historical and Mining Museum. Thank you, Ann. Dr. Chelton Feeny and Roger Green graciously took over my Thursday museum duties, so that I had more time to write. I am especially thankful for the books given to the museum by the National Park Service, which were loaded with valuable information.

It was a third grader from Fairbanks, Ivan Billings, who first encouraged me to write about the Alaska Pipeline as an engineering wonder. To convince me, he quickly sketched a cross section of an aboveground pipeline support system.

They say that Alaska is just a small town. Perhaps only in Alaska can you contact strangers to ask questions on tiny details of state history and know that you'll get a friendly answer. Reporter Tim Mowry of the *Fairbanks Daily News-Miner* took time from his busy schedule to promptly answer my email in regard to his summer 2004 article about ten fire-trapped river boaters. He remembered that after a helicopter rescue failed to come because of the thick smoke, the boaters floated the last 80-some miles of the creek and survived.

My husband Jon Gantenbein and our ward Stephen Finger deserve a big hug for their tremendous support during this endeavor. My time spent at the computer cut into my family time, and my collection of Alaska books outgrew our bookshelves. Jon and Stephen were a willing audience for my stories of natural disasters, battles, and madness. Fourteen-year-old Stephen eagerly read chapters and offered suggestions.

As I finish the manuscript, Stephen is canoeing the Yukon River. Along the way, he will see a riverboat graveyard, a gold rush ghost town, and active native fish camps. Every bend of the river has a human story. I know that the Adventure Alaska guide, high school teacher Joe Schumacher, will share some of those stories. The wild tales will fire Stephen's imagination.

I am grateful for the opportunity to share these twenty-eight Alaska stories with others.

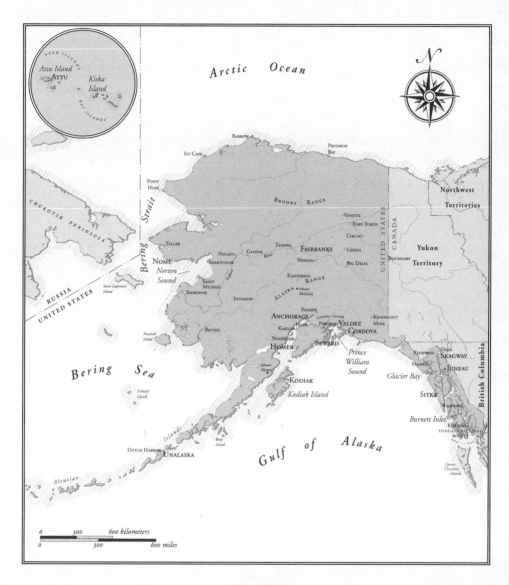

ALASKA

INTRODUCTION

The history of Alaska has been predominantly shaped by its geography. Its massive size, extreme landscape, and unpredictable weather have challenged and awed all those who ventured here. A map of Alaska reveals the bold character of this amazing land. The waters around the coast are peppered with islands, and great mountain ranges are slashed with mighty rivers. The names of these features flow off the tongue like music. Native words, such as Alyeska, Denali, Sitka, and Shaktoolik have a special beauty; while Russian place names like Baranof, Pribilof, and Kasilof have an Old World charm. Some communities boast names that originated during the gold rush frenzy, including Hope and Eureka. The names of other Alaskan towns have unusual, even serendipitous, histories. For instance, the town of "Nome" was inadvertently christened when a draftsman misread the phrase "No Name" on a map. Place names in Alaska have been complicated by the fact that the English alphabet does not convey the range of sounds in Russian and Native languages. As a result, linguists adjust the spelling every few decades, and historians struggle with the changes. I am guilty of choosing the simplest spellings, hoping the words will sing for everyone.

The human history of this great land began about 11,000 years ago, when early man walked across the Bering Land Bridge. The descendants of those first Native Alaskans have survived and developed distinct, rich cultures.

In the 1700s, Europeans found and exploited Alaska. Near the end of the century, the Russian-American Company beat down native Tlingit resistance at the Battle of Sitka and eventually enslaved

Aleuts to butcher fur seals on the Pribilof Islands. In the 1800s, however, the Russians could not control American whaling ships, which boldly ravaged the Alaskan seas. In 1867, Russia sold Alaska to America, thinking that most of the fur wealth was gone.

When Alaska became part of the United States, and after American explorers had learned what promise the land held, businessmen discovered new ways to make money in Alaska. The Americans found Alaskan treasures to fill their museums and libraries. Teams of scientists collected samples of plants and animals, and drew maps of the amazing landscape. Adventurous naturalist John Muir explored the glaciers and fjords.

With the invention of canning to preserve food, American companies fought to catch every Alaska salmon. Later, rumors of gold brought tens of thousands of newcomers rushing to the Last Frontier, with the dream of striking it rich in the gold fields. In 1897, "Klondike fever" electrified Alaska. Men fought over pokes of gold, copper mines, and railroad routes. Thousands worked to cut trails, roads, and railroads across the landscape. With the arrival of the railroad came a new vein to mine: tourism.

While the newcomers tried to conquer the land, the old Alaskans understood its power. The 1912 Mount Katmai eruption destroyed villages and dusted much of the Alaska Territory with gray ash. In addition, the 1913 conquest of Denali was a proud, yet humbling, moment for the four Alaskans who stood on her summit.

Over time, Americans interfered with Native Alaskan culture, depleting the wildlife and bringing new illnesses with them. Missionaries and government workers began to offer aid, usually with great fanfare. In the 1890s, one such experiment taught reindeer herding to Native Alaskans. Decades later, the U.S. government imported musk oxen for economic purposes. When a deadly diphtheria virus threatened Nome, a relay of dog sleds carried medicine across the heart of Alaska, saving the isolated town. The 1925 Serum Run was an Alaska-size drama!

During World War II, the Japanese took over Kiska and Attu islands, and American bombers blasted them for a year before winning them back. This man-made drama of 1942 was matched by nature twenty years later, when the 1964 Good Friday Earthquake shook the land and caused a great tsunami, hammering coastal communities.

When Alaska officially became a state in 1959, it was quickly realized that American policies and programs often interfered with the traditional lifestyle of Native Alaskans. In the 1960s, Inupiats in Barrow found a clever and peaceful way to protest an unfair hunting law. The resulting "Barrow Duck-In" spurred changes to the restrictive laws and allowed the Inupiats to continue their tradition of subsistence hunting. In the 1970s, the Molly Hootch Case successfully challenged the practice of sending native children to far-off boarding schools.

Following the Alaska Native Lands Settlement Act, the Alaska Oil Pipeline was laid on the tundra. The 800-mile pipeline, completed in 1977, was an engineering marvel. The 1989 Exxon Valdez Oil Spill, on the other hand, was a monumental human failure.

The Alaskan landscape captivates the imagination every March during the Iditarod Trail Sled Dog Race. Dog mushers take on the challenge of following the 1,049-mile Iditarod Trail across the heart of Alaska. The terrain is as extreme as the winter weather. *It Happened in Alaska* recalls a few of the amazing events that have taken place in the Great Land.

RUSSIANS MEET ALASKANS
ON THE ROCKS!

- 1741 -

The Aleutian Chain

THE MAP OF ALASKA RESEMBLES A FIST, with the thumb pointed down and the first finger extended. The thumb is the Alaska Panhandle, a long strip of land between Canada and the Pacific Ocean. The finger is the Aleutian Chain, a series of islands that stretches to Siberia. Above the chain is the Bering Sea.

In 1741 the Russian ship, *Saint Peter,* touched the Alaska Panhandle and traveled along the coast to the Aleutian Chain. On a small Aleutian island, Russians met Alaskan natives for the first time, and just like the coastal territory, this initial visit was rocky.

It was late May, and Russia's Great Northern Expedition had set sail from Siberia with the mission of reaching North America and claiming it for Russia. European mapmakers accepted the notion that the world was round, and the Russian emperor suspected that Siberia was close to the coast of North America.

The fleet was comprised of two ships and two cargo boats. Only a few short hours away from the harbor, the cargo boats crashed into each other and sank, along with most of the expedition's food and the boats' crews. Only five months' worth of food remained, and things quickly worsened. After a few days the two large ships separated in the fog. Each ship was alone and had to decide what it would do next. Independently, they both chose to continue sailing east. For the commander of the *Saint Peter*, Vitus Bering, this was the only option. He had failed to reach Alaska on his first expedition thirteen years earlier, and was determined to succeed this time or to die trying. However, most of the seventy-eight men aboard the *Saint Peter* wanted to quit. Bering pushed the crew to sail blindly across the wide Pacific Ocean, far south of the Aleutian Chain. For six weeks, they saw almost nothing.

Then, on July 15, 1741, to everyone's enormous relief, the *Saint Peter* sighted a grand, snow-covered mountain. The crew was overjoyed, and their thoughts of mutiny faded like the mist. Bering named the awesome peak Mount Saint Elias and claimed the mainland for Russia. They didn't know it then, but the other Russian ship had reached the top of the Alaska Panhandle.

A few crewmen, including the young naturalist, Georg Steller, rowed to a nearby island in search of fresh drinking water. While on land, Steller noticed smoke rising from a distant campfire. He hurried back to Commander Bering and requested permission to visit the natives, but was denied. Bering regretted having brought the disagreeable naturalist. To his way of thinking, they had completed the mission, and he hoped to be back in Siberia before winter came and their food ran out. He would stop for nothing but drinking water. The compass was set west and the *Saint Peter* sailed toward home along the relative safety of the coast. Bering did not want to venture across open water again. With luck they might live to see Siberia.

The long and troubled voyage soon took a turn for the worse. With a diet consisting largely of burnt biscuits, and lacking any vitamin C, Bering and half the crew began to suffer from scurvy. The ailment made the men very weak, and many of them suffered from bleeding gums and loose teeth. Georg Steller, in addition to being the ship's naturalist, was also the ship doctor, and believed that Alaskan berries could save their lives. However, Steller's know-it-all style annoyed his Russian shipmates, who ignored his advice. Bickering became the ship's other illness. The Russians cared little for Bering or his Swedish lieutenant, and the complaining became as problematic as the scurvy.

While the urge to return to Siberia was strong, the September headwinds were stronger, and the ship was nearly blown backwards. Unable to fight the wind in open water, the *Saint Peter* lowered her sails and anchored behind tiny Bird Island. Bering decided they would wait a few days and continue west after the winds died down. The rest would also be good for the sick men.

To their surprise, two small boats paddled up to the ship. These were one-man, sealskin-covered kayaks called bidarkas, both of which were about 12 feet long and very lean and graceful. The light crafts bobbed in the rough waters, yet the two Aleuts inside them seemed totally comfortable. They wore hooded, waterproof, seal-intestine parkas that were cinched around the lips of the boats to keep the paddlers dry. The Aleuts shouted loudly, but in a language Bering's crew could not understand. Georg Steller thought the boats resembled the kayaks that the Eskimos of Greenland built, but the men looked more Asian. Steller was impressed with their healthy appearance and suspected that they ate well. Speculating that the land and sea were rich in good things to eat, he hoped the Aleuts would share some of this food with the *Saint Peter*'s ill-fed sailors.

The Russians tied a gift of tobacco pipes and beads to a board and tossed this to one of the bidarkas. The Aleut in the other bidarka then held out a dead falcon on a stick, hoping a gift would be placed in the bird's claws. The sailor closest to him thought the Aleut wanted to come aboard. To help, he pulled on the bird, drawing the bidarka nearer the ship. The Aleut panicked and let go. Eventually the situation sorted itself out, and the Aleuts gestured that they were headed to Bird Island to get drinking water. The Russians were in need of more drinking water as well and decided to go ashore again.

Unfortunately, only a few were healthy enough to make the trip, including Georg Steller. Bering was in bed and was much too sick to go. After climbing into a longboat, the weak men struggled to row the short distance to the island. Great whitecaps rocked the boat and splashed over its sides. Fearing the boat would be shattered on the rocks, the men anchored offshore and waded naked across the icy water. On land they shivered in the biting September winds and pulled their warm, dry clothes back over their wet bodies.

Most of the island was visible from where they stood. The land was totally treeless, and the browning grass was blown flat. There was no village anywhere. A hunting party of Aleut men from another island greeted them. They wore warm fur pants and boots under their long, seal-gut parkas. Some carried iron knives, which Steller guessed they had crafted themselves. The friendly Aleuts offered the men whale blubber to eat, but the Europeans were hungry for familiar food and could not stomach the dense and chalky white fat.

The sailors who had ventured onto Bird Island were growing weary of the wind, which blew through their thin, worn clothing. They gave up on collecting drinking water, and began to gesture to the Aleuts about returning to the shelter of the ship. The Aleuts, however, had taken a keen interest in one particular member of the *Saint Peter* landing party—a Siberian Eskimo who was brown-skinned like them, but whose dress and language were very different. Several of the Aleuts held onto the Siberian, wanting him to stay, while a few others started to pull the Russians' wooden boat onshore. Both acts alarmed the Europeans, who started to worry that they were going to be held prisoner. Trying to gain control of the situation, three of the Russians fired muskets over the heads of the Aleuts. The Aleuts dropped to the ground in surprise. They had never seen or heard anything like this! Immediately the sailors made a dash for the longboat and rowed quickly back to the *Saint Peter*. No one was hurt, but the day was spoiled by misunderstandings. The Russians wanted to meet no more Aleuts on this trip, and the Aleuts would be wary of Europeans next time.

Soon the headwinds slackened and the *Saint Peter* was able to sail on, following the Aleutian Islands as their steppingstones to Siberia. The ship's sails frayed and ripped in the wind. Commander Bering was unable to rise from bed, and the crew grew weak as well. Twelve men died of scurvy, and only three remained healthy. In November the crew of the *Saint Peter* stopped to winter on an island off the coast of Siberia, which they named Bering Island. Thirty men, including Vitus Bering, died of scurvy that winter, and the anchored ship was blown into the rocks and destroyed.

As spring turned into summer, the remaining few men used the wreckage to build a new ship. Georg Steller was among the forty-six survivors who left Bering Island and sailed to Siberia in August of 1742. Fifteen months after it had begun, the ordeal was finally over. They had lost their ship, their leader, and nearly half the crew, but they had returned to Siberia.

Despite the many mishaps, Russia's Great Northern Expedition had accomplished its mission of reaching the Alaska mainland, and the explorers had even met Native Alaskans. The survivors brought back journals, notes, maps, and sketches. Based on what was learned, Russia laid claim to Alaska.

Though the men who met on that rocky coast are now long gone, the impact of their visit is still felt today. Two of the most important features on the map of Alaska bear Vitus Bering's name: the Bering Sea and the Bering Strait. Georg Steller's name is found in bird and mammal books. He was the first European to describe the Steller's sea cow, Steller's sea lion, Steller's jay, Steller's eider, Steller's eagle, and Steller's white raven. Perhaps more importantly, the Aleuts still call the Aleutian Islands home.

THE SEARCH FOR THE
NORTHWEST PASSAGE

- 1778 -

The Alaska Coastline

COULD A SHIP TRAVEL FROM THE ATLANTIC OCEAN across the top of
North America to the Pacific Ocean? In the eighteenth century, the
leaders of Europe wanted to know. If such a passage existed, then
the dangerous trip around the tip of South America could be
avoided and months could be shaved off the journey to the rich
Alaskan waters.

Two Russian expeditions, one in 1728 and the second in 1741,
had produced only rough maps of the North Pacific Ocean. The official 1774 Russian map showed "Alaskachka" as a huge island. The
area was still entirely unexplored by most European countries that
believed that there was very likely an ice-free Northwest Passage
across the top of North America. In 1776, Captain James Cook
intended to discover that passage. It would be Cook's third Pacific

voyage, and he planned to claim land for England and give English names to the landmarks he encountered on his quest.

Cook commanded the *Resolution,* and Charles Clerke captained its sister ship, the *Discovery.* Even the names of the vessels boldly declared their mission. The captains had been ordered not to waste time exploring the land, as this would slow them down and distract them from their ultimate purpose. All of the latest maps and books of the region were on board, as was an artist, who would draw this new world. No one spoke Russian, but this was not expected to pose a problem since they did not anticipate encountering any Russians on the trip in spite of that country's presence in the region.

After leaving England in 1776, they sailed to the Pacific Ocean. Roughly two years later, on May 1, 1778, Cook's crew spotted Alaska. The *Resolution* and *Discovery* sailed north along the Alaska Panhandle, where the deep green of the forests, the grand mountains, and the great cedar trees reaching up from the snow awed all aboard. Cook gave English names to some of the landmarks. Mount Edge-cumbe was named after a mountain in England, while Cape Fair-weather was named for the sunshine present when Cook first saw it. There were so many islands that Cook could not see the mainland. He believed they were passing an archipelago until he reached the mouth of what he hoped was a great passage.

While anchored at the mouth of this "passage," which Cook called Hinchenbrook Entrance, they met their first Native Alaskans. About twenty Alutiiqs paddled up in two round, skin-covered boats called umiaks. The Alutiiqs did not board the English ships, but gifts were tossed to them across the water. After the meeting the natives paddled off, singing as they went. Soon thereafter, the ships ventured into Hinchenbrook Entrance, but a storm forced them to anchor in an area they called Snug Corner Cove. As they waited out the storm, seven kayaks approached the English vessels, and their passengers—

Alutiiq men and women—boldly climbed aboard. Many had pierced upper lips, and some wore cone-shaped hats of woven grass. They gladly traded sea otter pelts for blue glass beads. To English eyes, the Alutiiqs looked very much like the Eskimos of Greenland, and the explorers were sure they had found a passage connecting Alaska to the waters of Greenland. When the weather cleared, they explored deep into the waterway, until eventually the land closed in and their hopes faded. Cook's supposed passage was actually the body of water later named Prince William Sound.

Sailing west out of the sound, the ships stopped at what looked like another great opening in the mainland. Again their hopes were raised; perhaps this was their Northwest Passage. It was only late May, and summer had hardly arrived, but Cook knew that the arctic summer was short and he still needed to sail the Northwest Passage to the Atlantic. As they sailed deeper into the waterway, it narrowed and looked more like a river. It was fed by fresh, but muddy, water. The channel appeared to split in two, so the ships anchored. A boat was sent to row up one fork and then the other. Both forks narrowed quickly, so the rowboat turned around and came back. With great disappointment, Cook decided that this was not his Northwest Passage, but nonetheless, he liked the look of the area. He decided to claim the land for England since it seemed to him like a good place to build an English town. A boat went ashore at Point Possession, which is across from present-day Anchorage, and they held a quick English ceremony on the beach. Sinking a flag in the soil, they claimed the land for the crown. Athabaskans watched the odd little show from a distance. The ships left Cook's great "river" in early June. These days we know this river as Cook Inlet.

Back in the open sea, the ships headed southwest to the Alaska Peninsula. Here, Alutiiqs paddled bidarkas across the water to the *Discovery.* Imagine the crew's surprise when the Alutiiqs produced a note written in Russian. Sadly, no one could read it. Later, another Alutiiq man came aboard, dressed in European clothes and bowing deeply like a European. This surprised the Englishmen even more. In addition, they soon met their first Aleuts, who kept saying the word "Russ" and showing with their hands that they wanted tobacco. They too presented Russian letters. It was becoming very clear to the Englishmen that the Russians had more than a passing acquaintance with the locals.

The ships' captains were pleased when they finally reached the western tip of the Alaska Peninsula. Here the long finger of land broke into islands, now called the Aleutian Chain. In late June the ships slipped north behind Unalaska Island. They took a few days to rest, studying this treeless island and visiting the village. Cook wrote about what he saw, noting that the Aleuts were short and plump. The men had small beards and wore seal-gut parkas over bird-skin suits. The women were beautiful and wore dresses of sea otter fur or seal-skin. The Englishmen were surprised to find that Aleut homes were mounds of earth called barabaras. The homes' design provided optimum protection from the winds; the shelter door was a hole in the roof that the Aleuts climbed down with the help of a notched-log ladder. Each barabara housed three or four families and was about 30 feet long by 15 feet wide.

Once the ships passed north of the Aleutians, they were in the Bering Sea. The *Resolution* and *Discovery* ventured east to broad Bristol Bay, which they named after a city in England. They put ashore at the far end of the bay at a place they named Cape Newenham, after an English nobleman. With British pomp they claimed the land for the king and left a bottle with a note saying so. Farther north, at Saint Matthew Island, they met Eskimos who wished to trade their furs. The Eskimos were not familiar with tobacco, the popular Russian trade good, and the Englishmen were sure this was the first time these Eskimos had ever met Europeans. The land of the Eskimos was different also. The shore was a flat, broad river delta where trees were scarce. To English eyes, the land was less beautiful than what they had viewed earlier. The land also looked less and less like the Russian maps they had brought with them.

The ships sailed past a large island, which Cook named King Island. At this point they were in the Bering Strait, where Alaska and Siberia are very close. Even though it was late August and winter was beginning to grip the arctic waters, Cook crossed the strait and visited Siberia. Returning to the Alaskan side, Cook was still hopeful when they passed what he called Point Hope, but hope faded as they entered what could only be named Icy Cape. Icebergs and walruses were everywhere. The men shot nine of the great beasts for the ships' cooks, and everyone was excited by the idea of fresh meat. However, even after four hours of boiling, the crew still hated the taste of walrus steaks. Open sea was becoming scarce, and the men were getting nervous as they watched the icepack closing in on them. The two ships were not built to battle icebergs, and sadly turned around, returning south through the Bering Strait. The search for a Northwest Passage was over for the year.

Both Cook and Clerke sailed south along the Alaskan coast, naming landmarks along the way. They stalled for a three-week rest on Unalaska Island. Captain Clerke was ill and needed to recover, and the ships had been damaged by icebergs and were in need of repair. Cook took advantage of the extra time on land and ordered some men to gather berries, as everyone needed the vitamin C in order to avoid scurvy. It was on Unalaska that the Englishmen met their first Russians. The island was home to a Russian trading post, which consisted of two storehouses and a bunkhouse. There were a few Russians at the trading post, but unfortunately they spoke no English and only limited French. Between French words and gestures, the Englishmen learned that these men made their living by traveling up and down the Aleutians, collecting sea otter pelts. The Russians said that in the early days, they had killed many Aleut leaders and taken away all weapons. Before long the Aleuts became so frightened of the Russians that they no longer fought back. A mere handful of Russians controlled all of the Aleuts.

Cook wished to draw a better map. The Russians could answer all of Cook's questions about the islands, but they knew little about the mainland. Cook added everything he learned from the Russians to what he had seen of the area himself and created a new map, giving one copy to the Russians. That winter, Captain Cook was killed in a bloody battle in the Hawaiian Islands. His ships, however, returned to Alaskan waters the next summer to look again for the Northwest Passage.

SLAVES OF THE SEAL HARVEST

- 1786 -

Pribilof Islands

CAPTAIN GERASIM PRIBILOF HAD SEARCHED for the fur seals' summer home for three years. For as long as anyone could remember, Russians had seen fur seals swim between Alaska's Aleutian Islands, heading north. But where did the seals go, and why couldn't Pribilof find them?

In 1786, while Pribilof was exploring the Bering Sea for his third summer, fog surrounded his ship, the *Saint George,* and the Russian crew could see virtually nothing. Pribilof decided not to set the anchor, and for a few days the ship drifted in the current while he waited for the fog to lift. One day a few of the men began to hear something—a roar they couldn't quite identify. Before long they all recognized it, and with growing excitement Pribilof ordered the crew to sail toward the sound of barking seals. As the ship drew closer to the noise, an island emerged through the mist, now known as Saint

George Island. The beach was alive with hundreds of thousands of seals. At last, they had found their seal island.

The men anchored and went ashore to find a treeless island, entirely devoid of human life. A few sailors and supplies were left behind to explore Saint George for the entire nine-month winter, while most of the crew returned to the relative comfort of a Russian outpost in the Aleutians. Those left behind would have to hunt their own food and create their own shelter from driftwood and sod. They prayed that they'd be rescued the following summer.

Fortunately for them, Pribilof did return the next summer. The men reported that they had discovered a sister island, also uninhabited, during their long winter. They named it Saint Paul Island. These two islands, plus two tiny ones called Walrus and Otter, were collectively named the Pribilof Islands. They are located in the middle of the Bering Sea, about 200 miles north of the Aleutian Islands.

During the 1700s, Russians sought warm Alaskan furs to sell to the Chinese, who were happy to pay high prices for them. At first, they hunted the Alaska sea otter. When the otter was almost gone, the Russians turned their attention to the Alaska fur seal. While the Russians were good trappers of land animals, they were poor hunters of sea mammals. However, they knew that Native Alaskans had hunted these animals for generations, and decided they needed the skilled Aleuts to help them hunt, even if it meant enslaving them.

The Aleuts made their home in Alaska's Aleutian Chain, a 1,000-mile-long string of islands. In the early 1700s, there may have been as many as 25,000 Aleuts living there. In fact, this was the most heavily populated part of Alaska. At that time, the ocean was thick with sea mammals and fish; the treeless, volcanic islands were rich with good things to eat; and the cliffs were home to millions of seabirds. The Aleuts had harvested from the land and sea for generations.

They were good warriors, but they knew nothing of guns since they had never had altercations with outsiders before.

An early incident in the Aleutians had set the pattern for Russian-Aleut interaction, which was very much in effect when Captain Pribilof found the islands that bear his name. In 1745, Russians stopped at an island, intending to kidnap native women. The Aleut community invited them to stay and feast, but when the guests tried to leave with their women, the Aleut men objected. The Russians raised their muskets and fired into the crowd, killing fifteen men and taking the women. This was the first killing of Aleuts by Russians, but it was not the last. The Russians terrorized this and other islands for years. After roughly twenty years of such violence, the Aleuts almost never fought back. They paid taxes to the Russians in furs, work, and money. Wives and children were held hostage in order to convince Aleut men to hunt for furs. By the late 1700s, the Aleuts were little more than slaves of the Russians.

Captain Pribilof was employed by the Russian-American Company, which was no better than any of the other Russian companies in terms of how it treated the Aleuts. Each spring, his company brought Aleut hunters to the Pribilof Islands. At first, the men stayed for just the summer, harvesting seals. In the fall, those who had managed to endure the constant labor, poor food, and primitive living conditions were returned to their Aleutian villages. After a few years, sod-house villages were built on the Pribilof Islands, and the hunters stayed year-round. Aleut wives were allowed to join their husbands, and children were born.

At harvest time, the Aleut men walked among the seals on the rocky beach, taking care not to be bitten by the animals' sharp teeth. Some men were "stunners"—they raised a wooden club and brought it down on the head of a seal, crushing the animal's thin skull. The seal died quickly, and the man moved on to kill another. Next, a "ripper" cut along the belly and flippers of the warm seal body. The carcass was pinned to the ground, and three men grabbed the hide and pulled it off of the dead seal. A broad knife was scraped up and down the hide to remove the blubber, after which the hide was rubbed with salt. Each skin weighed about ten pounds. Hundreds of them were loaded aboard each Russian ship, and many thousands were shipped to China and traded for tea.

The Russian government suspected that the fur companies were killing too many fur seals, just as they had nearly killed all of the sea otters. In an effort to gain some control of the situation, one company, the Russian-American Company, was given total control of Alaska in 1799. The Russian government asked that the company treat the Aleuts fairly, but with no government officials overseeing their actions, the company ignored this rule. Four out of five Aleut men were forced to harvest seals for little money or food. The Pribilof Aleuts all but forgot how to kayak and perform other basic skills. Russian food items like sugar and tea became part of their diet. Slowly, the Aleuts took Russian names and learned to speak Russian.

In 1824, an Orthodox Christian priest arrived in the Aleutian Islands. Sent by the Russian government, he announced that baptized Aleuts did not have to pay Russian taxes for three years. Naturally, many Aleuts thought this was a good reason to join the church. Additionally, the church treated the Aleuts with respect, which they also liked. Over time, the priest studied the Aleut language and devised the first Aleut alphabet. Likewise, Aleuts continued to learn Russian, and they were taught how to read the Bible and follow the mass. Eventually churches were built in the center of the villages and became a key part of village life. A few Aleuts were sent to Russia for schooling, returning home as priests and teachers. In the mid-1800s, the Russian-American Company began employing educated Aleuts as bosses and storekeepers.

Many Aleuts died between 1741 and 1867, the years when Russians enslaved them as fur hunters. In all of the Aleutian Islands, there were never more than 400 Russians; the Aleuts did most of the work. In addition, the best hunters were taken from two Aleutian Islands for years, and the villagers who were left behind had to struggle to feed themselves. The Russians also brought with them new diseases which devastated the Aleut population. By the 1860s, there were less than 2,000 Aleuts left in the Aleutian Islands.

Along with the shrinking Aleut population came a shrinking seal population. Eventually the Russian government became worried enough to impose conservation rules on the Russian-American Company. The declining seal trade was a major reason why Russia decided to sell Alaska to the United States in 1867, at a cost of $7.2 million.

Interestingly, American politicians believed the country could earn back the money by sealing, even though the Russians were no longer profitable at it. The first American contract for seal harvesting was given to the Alaska Commercial Company. Things changed little for the Pribilof Aleuts, as they were still harvesting seals, being paid in food, and not free to leave the island. The situation on the Pribilofs bore some resemblance to the system of slavery that the United States had just fought the Civil War to end.

Reforms occurred slowly on the Pribilofs. The Pribilof hunters were later paid in company store tokens and finally in American money. It wasn't until the 1960s that the Pribilof Aleuts could travel from the islands without obtaining official permission. In 1983, the U.S. government declared an end to the seal harvest. Aleuts could still hunt seals for their own dinner, a practice called subsistence hunting, but they needed a new way to make money. Some became commercial fishermen and others became tour guides. Today, Saint Paul Aleuts take visitors to the rookeries to watch the noisy drama of seal life.

THE BATTLE OF SITKA

- 1802 & 1804 -

Sitka

IN JUNE 1802, MASKED TLINGIT WARRIORS crept through the spruce forest to the Russian settlement of New Archangel. Moving stealthily alongside the Sitka Tlingit were warriors from other Tlingit tribes, intent on destroying this tiny colony and taking back the Alaska Panhandle. The Russians had worn out their welcome.

The Alaska Panhandle is a beautiful strip of coastline and large islands with towering cedar trees where the surrounding water is rich with salmon and sea otters. Long before the Russians arrived, the Tlingits had built permanent villages of huge wooden houses. Grand totem poles and large war canoes displayed their fine carving skills. The Tlingits had traded with other natives for generations and had recently begun to trade with American ships. Americans stayed only briefly and traded firearms for furs, an arrangement the Tlingits liked. In fact, after only a short time of trading with Americans, the Tlingits had a large supply of guns. A very proud people, the Tlingits were losing patience with these visitors to the Alaska Panhandle, the Russians. They were rude, brought their own native slave hunters, and refused to trade for firearms.

Three years earlier, in 1799, Russian ships had sailed into Sitka Sound, with Aleuts piloting 300 bidarkas alongside them. The Aleuts were Russian-American Company employees, slaves really, and Alexander Baranof was their chief manager. For fifty years, the Russian company had hunted sea otters in the Aleutian Chain and Kodiak Island waters until there were few of them left. Then the company turned its attention to the sea otters in the water along the Alaska Panhandle.

Baranof left one of the two ships and boldly walked into the Sitka village. He presented the Sitka Tlingit chief with gifts of beads, bottles, and brass; and for this the Tlingits reluctantly gave him the piece of land he requested, 6 miles from the village. Baranof declared that the land would be the site of a new colonial city, which he named New Archangel. He stayed at this site only a short time, and left behind 300 Russians and Aleut men, women, and children to finish building the community. In three years, they constructed a few crude log buildings, including a warehouse, which they filled with sea otter pelts that the Aleuts had harvested. Of course, according to the Tlingits, the outsiders had no right to hunt otters in Tlingit waters, but should have been trading for those furs, preferably in guns.

In addition to the warehouse and other buildings, the Russians and Aleuts were constructing a ship on the beach. The Tlingits were amused by the cows that Baranof had left, but they were far from amused by the Russians. The intruders had imprisoned a Tlingit man, taken Tlingit women, and robbed Tlingit graves. By 1802, the Tlingits would no longer tolerate the Russians, and a plan was hatched.

On that infamous June morning in 1802, while some Tlingit warriors hid in the woods surrounding New Archangel, other Tlingits in war canoes paddled up the sound. At midday, the two forces rushed the settlement with a single, blood-curdling scream. The Russians and Aleuts were greatly outnumbered. A few Aleut women and their crying children were quickly captured, and most colonists fled to the log barracks, the only two-story building. Bolting the door behind them, they climbed upstairs and watched from the windows as the Tlingits torched the lower logs of their shelter. As the flames began to spread upward, some of the colonists became frantic and jumped from the burning building—only to be skewered on upright spears set in the earth below. Horrified, others huddled together and burned to death. After the Tlingit warriors took all of the otter pelts from the warehouse, they set fire to it, along with most other structures. As the settlement blazed, the surviving Aleut women and children were carried off to the Sitka village.

When all of this started, a few Russians and Aleuts had been in the woods, picking berries. When they heard the war cries, they crouched down in the bushes and heard the final ghastly screams of over 250 of their comrades. For hours they watched the flames of New Archangel rise higher and higher. Eventually the fire died away and New Archangel was nothing but ashes.

The hidden Russians and Aleuts could see there was nothing left of their colony, and what had once been their home was now hostile territory, hundreds of miles from the nearest Russian post. What could they do? They started walking away, down the dark and dangerous beach. Days later, an English ship picked up the stragglers and took them to the Russian-American Company's fur trading post on Kodiak Island. However, the English captain stopped acting as a rescuer and started acting as a hostage-taker: he aimed his cannons at the company and demanded a large ransom for the twenty-three

New Archangel survivors he had onboard. Only three of the hostages were Russian men, and most of the Aleuts were women. Alexander Baranof, who happened to be at the trading post at the time, hated having to pay for anyone's freedom, but he especially hated having to buy back Aleut women. Nonetheless, he paid.

Although his colony was gone, along with his supply of furs, Baranof was not defeated. In fact, he still wanted to establish the Russian-American Company fur trading headquarters in Sitka Sound. This time he intended to destroy Sitka village and replace it with a Russian post. A small man with a huge ego, Baranof was intent on revenge and not about to have his plans foiled by anyone.

Two years later, in the summer of 1804, the Sitka Tlingits saw two Russian ships sail into Sikta Sound. Their old enemy was back. Expecting a fight, the Tlingits quickly built a fort near the beach, stocking it with guns and ammunition. The entire community— men, women, and children—moved into the fort. Over the course of several weeks, three more Russian ships arrived in Sitka Sound. Baranof was aboard one of the smaller ones. The largest ship, the *Neva,* was a warship with several cannons and a super-strong hull. Along with the ships were 800 Aleuts paddling 300 bidarkas. It took one hundred Aleut bidarkas just to tow the *Neva* into position across from the fort. The *Neva* aimed its cannons at the Tlingits, ready to do battle.

Baranof and a few others came ashore in bidarkas. Some of his men stationed themselves on steep Castle Hill, while the Aleuts took position on the hillside. The Tlingits watched and worried, seeing no way they could win. The chief and some of his warriors came out of the fort and signaled to Baranof and his men that they wanted to discuss peace. Baranof's terms, however, were too much: he demanded they hand over the village of Sitka and a few Tlingit hostages. The Tlingits shook their heads and returned to the fort, bracing for the battle to come. From Castle Hill, Baranof's men began to shoot volleys at the fort. Most of the bullets fell short of their target and did little damage. Impatient, Baranof led a night attack on the fort, thinking he could creep closer under cover of darkness. This was a mistake. Tlingit warriors boldly left the fort and battled Russians and Aleuts on the beach. The Tlingits were fearless in the hand-to-hand fighting that followed. Ten of Baranof's men were killed and another twenty-four were wounded. Baranof's right arm was injured so badly that he could no longer fight. Wisely, he turned over command of the battle to the *Neva's* captain.

From the ship, the captain ordered the cannons to resume firing. They pounded the fort with cannon balls. A Tlingit war canoe was sighted in the sound, paddling swiftly toward the fort. It was loaded with gunpowder. After Tlingits dragged the great canoe onshore, a cannonball hammered it and the boat's cargo of gunpowder exploded instantly, throwing pieces of canoe everywhere. The fort had no ammunition left, and thirty warriors lay dead inside its walls. The crew of the *Neva,* feeling victorious, raised a flag on its mast. Those in the fort attached a piece of white fabric to the top of a pole in response, unaware that a white flag is the European symbol of surrender. As the Russians understood it, the Tlingits had given up and the Battle of Sitka was over.

For three days, Baranof and the Tlingit chief attempted to come to terms. Communication depended on very poor translators and hand gestures, so the negotiations were confusing. Yet the Tlingits were unwilling to declare defeat. On the fourth morning of the negotiations, the fort was quiet and the Tlingits did not come forth. Before long, the Russians entered to investigate. Inside the fort, they found two old women with five dead children. The Russians were totally surprised to discover that the rest of the village had escaped. Since a silent escape would have been impossible with crying little ones, the Tlingits had killed their own children before fleeing into the woods. Baranof was bitter, as he had won only half a victory: the Russians had Sitka, but no Tlingit slaves. The next day the Russians set fire to the Sitka fort. The flames rose skyward, and with the flames went Tlingit control of their land, water, and trade.

Baranof built a Russian post near the ashes of the Sitka Tlingit fort and again named his post New Archangel, as proof that the Russians had indeed won. The settlement became the headquarters of his Russian-American Company, and Baranof stayed and commanded the entire company before retiring and leaving Alaska in 1818. Over time, New Archangel grew to be a refined city of nearly 2,000. Some called it the "Paris of the Pacific." The Sitka Tlingits, at first dispersed through the island, trickled back to live on the perimeter of the Russian city. Tlingits, and visiting Americans, continued to call it by its old name, Sitka.

Today, the city is officially called Sitka, and Sitka National Historical Park rangers guide visitors to the different battle landmarks. The Sitka-Tlingit tribe, Sheet'ka, also offers tours of their homeland. On these tours they share their cultural memory of New Archangel and the Battle of Sitka.

LITTLE GIRL ON A
BERING SEA WHALER

- 1857 -

Bering Sea

A Bering Sea whaler was a floating factory, slippery with blubber and blood. It was a dangerous place for a little girl to play with her doll. Yet, in 1857, six-year-old Minnie Lawrence was aboard such a whaler.

In late 1856, Minnie traveled with her mother, Mary, and her father, Captain Samuel Lawrence, to Alaska on his whaling ship, the *Addison*. Their home was New Bedford, Massachusetts, where whaling was the leading business. Captain Lawrence had been away, whaling in the Pacific, for most of Minnie's first five years. Minnie's mother was a spirited young woman who was tired of being home alone. She wanted to spend some time with her husband and see Alaska for herself. She also wanted Minnie to get to know her father better. Mary and Samuel decided that mother and daughter would travel along for a single whaling trip. This would give the family quite a reunion, since whaling voyages could last for years.

A whaling ship did not look like other ships. The *Addison* was only slightly over 100 feet long. It was strong, but fat and slow. On the deck was a great brick oven with two 100-gallon kettles for boiling blubber. Most ships had six whaleboats, and each of these 30-foot boats had space for four oarsmen, a harpooner, a boat officer, and 2,000 pounds of blubber. They also carried rope, harpoons, spears, and a bomb gun. These six whaleboats were the workhorses of the *Addison*'s whaling expedition.

The *Addison* set sail with a crew of thirty-two; everyone lived below deck. The Lawrence family had a nice stateroom, but there was only one kitchen on board, the galley. The first cook would not let Mary use his oven, and so the Lawrences had to eat whatever was being served to the entire crew, which wasn't always an appetizing concoction. Not long after the ship left Massachusetts, the cook fell ill and died. His replacement, who hadn't really signed on to this adventure to cook, cared more for whaling than cooking. He was happy to let Mary prepare meals for the entire ship when he was needed elsewhere. On stopovers in Hawaii, Mary stocked up on a wonderful variety of meats, fruits, and vegetables. These were a daily part of family meals and were sometimes shared with the crew.

Minnie enjoyed growing up on the ship. A few pigs and chickens ran loose on the deck, and Minnie gave them names like Wiggie and Pinkie and chased them around. The sailors sang sea songs and she joined in. Minnie's dark hair was cut chin length and her dress hung just below her knees, covering her white pantaloons. This style gave her more freedom than the long hoop skirt her mother wore. Minnie was a good mother to her china doll, Sarah Price, and she even had her own little tub on washday for her doll's dress.

It took the *Addison* five months to reach its goal—the waters of Alaska. These waters were the bowhead whale's summer playground, and the *Addison* was one of 143 Alaskan whalers that summer in search of the bowhead. Alaska belonged to Russia, but since Russia had no whaling fleet of her own, Americans were free to kill thousands of Alaska's whales and anchor at any Alaska island they wished.

The killing of whales was gruesome, but it was also exciting. Mary and Minnie watched their first whale hunt in awe. One of the sailors was always aloft, watching for whales, and early in the day a sailor spotted one. The whaleboats were immediately dropped into the water, but before the men could get into position, the whale dove. The men waited anxiously for the great mammal to come up for air, wondering if they would have to frantically row after it or be ready to use their weapons. On this first day, the whale rose just a few yards away, and the boat officer ordered the harpooner to fire. With as much luck as skill, the sharp point sank into the flesh, squirting blood. The angry beast strained and thrashed, but the harpoon was tied to the boat. After a moment of trying to dislodge the harpoon, the whale swam toward open sea, dragging the boat behind it. For Minnie, this was one of the scariest moments in the hunt; she was frightened that the whale would pull forever and the men would disappear over the edge of the horizon. Mary, on the other hand, thought it would be even worse if the whale flipped the boat, sending the men into the frigid water. While the first boat was being pulled, another boat shot a second harpoon. The whale, red with blood, smacked its great tail on the surface of the ocean, sending water and blood shooting into the air. Another boat joined the fight. As the great animal tired, the boats closed in, shortening their lines. Afraid to get too close, the men fired off a shot. The shell hit the whale and exploded, sending blubber and blood everywhere. Once the animal was dead, the mass was dragged back to the ship. Mary and Minnie gaped at the enormity of the ravaged animal—their minds adjusting to accommodate the unimaginable size of it.

Mary had never given much thought to what happened to the whale after it was caught, but she soon learned that butchering was dirty, smelly work. The whale carcass, which was 65 feet long, was held tight to the ship with one chain around the tail and another snaked through the blowhole and out his mouth. A man stood on the slippery body and hacked at the spine with an axe, blood and oil spraying back with each stroke. Minnie was terribly afraid because she realized that the whale's blood drew sharks. Looking around, she counted six of them. The man who was attacking the whale's spine kept slipping, and Minnie knew that if he lost his footing, he would fall to the sharks.

After hours of gruesome work, the great head hung free of its body. Pails were lowered down, and men climbed into the head, dipping out oil by the bucketful. When drained, the head was dragged on deck. With the body still tied to the ship, men climbed around, cutting the blubber into strips. The white, dense fat, which was 8 inches thick, peeled off easily. The dead whale was turned at least twice before it was totally stripped. Then the skeleton and guts were dropped to the sharks. On deck, the blubber and tongue were chopped up and tossed into the boiling pots. Smoke blew everywhere. All of the oil was poured into barrels; the body of a large bowhead whale could be boiled down to 275 barrels of oil, which would be used for candles and lamp fuel. The baleen, which some whales have instead of teeth, was the other prized part of a whale. Baleen looks like extremely long black feathers. It was ripped from the jaw and rinsed free of blood before being packed in bundles. This bowhead yielded 3,500 pounds of baleen, a few strips of which would eventually be added to some fine lady's corset to make it stiff. Mary and Minnie soon learned that on a good day, the crew might kill two or three whales before they started to butcher, and that one whale took the crew up to three days to finish.

Although their mission was to catch whales, sometimes the ship stopped to investigate Alaska and its people. Anchoring at Unalaska Island in the Aleutians, Mary and Minnie went ashore. It felt good to walk on solid ground, and they were delighted with the colors of the treeless, volcanic island: red rock, green grass, and a wealth of wildflowers. On one hillside they stopped to eat strawberries, blackberries, and huckleberries, and they carried a great armful of flowers back to the ship. On occasion, Native Alaskans paddled to the *Addison* and climbed aboard. Mary and Minnie enjoyed each visit, even though no one could penetrate the language barrier. Little Minnie tried to talk with them, which made them laugh. Still, it was fun to see different faces and try to understand each other. For many natives, this was the first time they had ever seen a white woman and girl.

When autumn rolled into winter, the *Addison* headed south and the Lawrences and the crew spent four months in Hawaii. After the crew was rested and their spirits were restored by the gorgeous Hawaiian Islands, the ship headed back to Alaskan waters in early spring. In the summer of 1858, the *Addison* hit an iceberg. Mary and Minnie turned the event into an adventure. While carpenters repaired the hull, the Lawrence family had fun visiting with other ships' officers.

The *Addison* returned to Massachusetts in 1860 with a fair haul: 27,187 pounds of baleen and 2,442 barrels of oil. After the bills were paid, there was almost $150,000 in profit—a lot of money! Of this, Captain Lawrence received $12,500. In comparison, the cabin boy earned only $180. Of the original crew, only nine returned to Massachusetts. Two had drowned, seven had deserted, and fourteen had quit. The golden age of Alaskan whaling was from 1835 to 1860.

Fewer ships whaled during the Civil War because the ships were needed for the war effort. Perhaps more importantly, people started filling their lamps with petroleum around 1880, and also around this time ladies stopped wearing baleen corsets. The whaling era was over. While New Englanders missed those glory days, the legacy in Alaska was of depleted whale populations that resulted in entire native villages starving to death for lack of blubber.

The Lawrence family never went whaling again after their return to Massachusetts in 1860. Captain Lawrence switched to Atlantic Ocean steamships, starting with a Union Army steamer. In the 1880s, Mary Lawrence loaned her diary to a writer, and it became the basis of a novel, *A Good Catch*. Minnie returned home as an adventurous nine-year-old. Her life was somewhat solitary as she remained an only child and never married, but she maintained her adventurous spirit. As an adult, she wrote poetry and told stories, and as an old woman, Minnie amused large crowds with tales of Bering Sea whaling.

REBEL RAIDERS IN THE BERING SEA

- 1865 -

Bering Sea

FAR FROM THE MASON-DIXON LINE AND THE battlefields of Virginia, the last blow of the Confederacy during the Civil War took place in Alaska's Bering Sea. The Confederate crew relished their victory—until they learned that it had taken place ten weeks after the war had ended.

In October of 1864, Confederate Commander James Waddell had been instructed to damage or destroy every Yankee whaling ship in the Pacific Ocean. His steamer *Shenandoah* was essentially a pirate ship, intent on cutting off one of the Union's most important financial resources: whaling. If Northern housewives were unable to buy whale oil candles to light their homes, it was a bonus. Hopefully, fuel shortages would stir anti-war sentiment in the Union. Sailing to Alaska and single-handedly taking on a fleet of whalers was a risky and slow proposition, but the Confederates needed to think big. The Confederate Army was suffering tremendous losses on the battlefield, and the Confederate Navy was tiny. By secretly purchasing the British Isles' fastest cruiser and destroying the Yankee whaling fleet, there was still a chance that the South might win. Commander Waddell felt a personal pleasure in the mission as well, since he hated the Yankees with a passion.

From the British Isles the *Shenandoah* headed east, rounding the tip of Africa and racing to the Alaskan whaling grounds. This king of ships could cruise 320 miles a day. It was 220 feet long with three masts, two coal-burning steam engines, six massive cannons, and two small saluting cannons cast in bronze to resemble lions. The warship's optimum crew was 150, yet it started its journey with only forty-three Confederates and European mercenaries. As it proceeded, the *Shenandoah* picked up over forty volunteers in Australia and several Yankee captives switched sides. The ship carried a Confederate flag and a variety of other flags; they would fly whichever one they needed in order to draw close to Yankee ships. Before even reaching their destination, they captured fourteen Yankee commercial ships. The majority of these were whaling ships, and most were burned.

Waddell and his crew felt invincible. They were closing in on their prey and they had had unexpected success in taking those first fourteen ships, which fueled their confidence and resolve. Unfortunately, the British Isles are extremely far from Alaska, and it had taken them six months to obtain the *Shenandoah* and sail to the Pacific Ocean. The Civil War was over before the warship even reached Alaskan waters. General Lee had surrendered on April 9, 1865, but it would be many weeks before this news reached the Rebel raiders in the Bering Sea.

The crew was recovering from a drinking binge when the *Shenandoah* reached the Bering Sea. They had captured a Yankee whaler off the southern coast of Siberia, and the vessel's cargo included over thirty barrels of whiskey. The victors broke into the stock and had many toasts to the burning whaler, *Abigail.* The captain, and a few other crewmembers who had remained sober, pushed the ship ahead of a storm and into the Bering Sea.

In mid-June, the northern waters were thick with New England whaling ships. There were fifty-eight in the Bering Sea and Arctic Ocean. Most were happy to be far from the Civil War, and although this was Russian territory, the Yankees expected no interference from any government ships. They habitually approached new ships to socialize and swap news. The whalers were fat, slow factory vessels, and each whaler was lucky to have even thirty-five men. They never stood a chance against the fastest ship in the sea. Destroying Yankee whalers proved easier than catching turtles in a pail.

The *Shenandoah*'s usual strategy was to display a false flag. After they were close to the Yankee ship, the Southern Cross was hoisted and a signal cannon fired a warning shot. The Yankee crews were always surprised by the ploy. They had no cannons, only whale harpoons and bomb guns. A Confederate boarding party captured most ships without firing a single bullet, and no one was killed. The victors looted the captured vessels for food, water, and valuables, and then the whaling crews were taken as prisoners and most of the ships were burned. The whale oil and precious baleen went up in smoke. It was demoralizing for the Yankees to watch a few years' work destroyed in hours, but what could they do? They were outmanned and outgunned. At one point the *Shenandoah* had so many captives that 200 of them had to be towed behind in twelve whaleboats.

On her first day in the Bering Sea, June 24, more than two months after the end of the war, the *Shenandoah* seized her first whalers. Both were large vessels, heavy with whale oil and baleen, and worth a small fortune.

The second day in the Bering Sea was even more fruitful. Five fat whaling ships were up against an ice floe. When they saw an American flag fluttering from the *Shenandoah*'s mast, they assumed it was sailing for the new Western Union Telegraph Expedition. The *Milo* drew over for a friendly "hello," and its captain was shocked to find that he immediately became a Confederate prisoner. He informed his captors that the Civil War was over, but Commander Waddell was sure he was bluffing, and the *Milo*'s captain had no newspaper to prove otherwise. The *Shenandoah* captured all five whaling vessels that day. Four of the ships were burned, and the prisoners were loaded onto the *Milo* and sent to San Francisco for ransom.

On June 26, the Rebel raiders took a New England whaler and a San Francisco trading ship named the *Susan Abigail,* which was bound for Siberia with whiskey and tobacco. The Confederates helped themselves to the cargo before torching the ships. On the fourth day of the campaign, June 27, six Yankee whalers were taken. Again, the Rebels burned five of the ships and loaded the sixth one with prisoners bound for San Francisco.

June 28 saw the biggest and last *Shenandoah* attack. With an American flag flying, the warship approached and took ten ships. The captain of the *Favorite* challenged the Rebels with a whaling gun. Little did he know that his crew had already abandoned ship, disabling the bomb gun before leaving. Finding the gun useless, the captain waved a sword at the warship while taking swigs from a bottle of whiskey. When the Confederates finally came aboard the *Favorite,* the captain was too drunk to be a threat. In a campaign that had met little resistance, the crew voted this Yankee the bravest they had captured. He was held in irons in order to thwart whatever escape attempt his drunken mind could cook up.

Another of the ships taken that day was the *James Murray.* When the Confederates boarded it, they were startled to find a woman in charge. Her husband, the captain, had died earlier in the voyage, and she was keeping watch over her three young children and one large barrel. The barrel held her husband's body, pickled in whiskey. She refused to let anyone drink the booze or feed her husband to the sharks. She begged that her ship be spared from the torch. The *James Murray* and the *Nile* were loaded with some 500 Yankee prisoners. While eight ships were burned, these two set sail for San Francisco, again to be offered for ransom.

Even in June there is ice in the Bering Sea, and navigating through it in the fog, with the accompanying thumps and bumps against the hull, was unnerving to Waddell. At one point, he had to send sailors out to hack the ship out of an ice floe. Waddell had had enough. He turned the *Shenandoah* around and headed south. After squeezing through the Aleutian Islands, he sought a newspaper so he could learn how the war was going. It was on August 2 when the last active Confederate unit learned that the Civil War had been over for nearly four months.

In five days, the *Shenandoah* had captured twenty-four whaling ships in the Bering Sea. Twenty were burned, while four ships and about 800 sailors were held for ransom. All of this damage was done in the name of the Confederacy after the Civil War was over. Nonetheless, the Confederates gained some satisfaction in knowing that the New England whaling industry was crippled. Massachusetts's leading whaling port, New Bedford, had lost nearly all of its whaling vessels, and the Bering Sea whaling fleet never returned to its 1850s strength. The golden age of Yankee whaling was over.

SCIENCE AND MADNESS ON
THE YUKON RIVER

- 1865 -

Yukon River

IN 1861, AMERICA HAD STRETCHED A TELEGRAPH WIRE from the Atlantic states to California. Now the nation was eager to be connected to Europe. Unfortunately, the first attempt to lay a telegraph wire across the Atlantic Ocean had failed, and the notion of laying wire across that enormous body of water was feeling more and more far-fetched to the engineers who had attempted it. All eyes turned to the Pacific Ocean, which was less than 60 miles wide in the Bering Strait. Why not stretch a telegraph wire from Alaska to Siberia and overland to Europe?

In August 1865, Major Robert Kennecott stepped off a ship at the mouth of the Yukon River. Just thirty years old, he had the frail good looks of a romantic poet. His Western Union Telegraph Company Expedition uniform had the same false military polish as his title, but his formal garb contrasted in an interesting manner with the Indian moccasins he wore on his feet. Kennecott nervously rushed back and forth as supplies were unloaded onto the beach. Had everything he purchased in San Francisco made it to Alaska? Was his crew cheating him? Did they want the mission to fail? Were his men out to kill him? Paranoid and suspicious thoughts had been creeping into Kennecott's mind ever since he had left San Francisco.

Before Kennecott set out, the Western Union Telegraph Company had contracted with Russia to lay wire in Russian America (now Alaska) and Siberia. In addition, the Canadian government had granted permission to lay American telegraph wire in western Canada. Once all the paperwork was signed, the pressure was on to complete the line quickly. Western Union knew it was only a matter of time before another company succeeded with a transatlantic line. Robert Kennecott was quickly hired as chief of the company's Russian–American division. His employers decided to give him the military title "Major" to set the tone for the expedition, and to show his crew that he would lead with a firm hand.

Robert Kennecott was selected because he was the only United States citizen known to have traveled the Yukon River. He was a naturalist and a loner, who had canoed across western Canada, including a few hundred miles of the Yukon River. He had also spent a full winter in cold, remote Fort Yukon. These credentials were enough for Western Union. Even though Kennecott's excellent fieldwork had always been conducted alone, and even though his superiors thought he had seemed nervous and uneasy, he was selected to direct their team.

In San Francisco, Western Union hired over forty men to accompany Kennecott and handle the telegraph work. Some were truly lazy, but Kennecott distrusted all of them. He was sure that his second-in-command was slowing things down to make him look bad to the company.

The expedition's Scientific Corps was solely Kennecott's idea. As head of that group, he chose six other scientists, including experts on plants, insects, birds, fish, mammals, and dinosaurs. There was also an artist to sketch and paint the landscape. Kennecott watched enviously as members of the Scientific Corps were set free to explore when and where they chose, taking notes and collecting samples, while he stayed near the ship.

Once all of the supplies, provisions, and belongings were on the beach, the crew became worried. Kennecott had not brought enough food to feed an expedition of fifty men for at least a year. There were only 6,000 pounds of food, and it was mostly flour. If the men were to labor in sub-zero weather, they needed much more. They feared it would be a hungry winter.

A Russian trading post, Saint Michael, sat where the Yukon River flowed into the Bering Sea. The expedition set up camp on the beach below the blockhouse, a prominent Russian guard structure. Kennecott sent half of the men and supplies north. Their mission was to explore the coastline up to where the Bering Strait was so narrow that one could see Siberia, and then begin setting telegraph poles in the ground, working their way backward from the Bering Strait down the coast to Saint Michael. Kennecott led the other men up the 2,000-mile Yukon River, where they would locate the ideal telegraph right-of-way. Then they too were to set telegraph poles, beginning at the Canadian end of the Yukon River and working back toward the coast. Hopefully these two lines would connect at Saint Michael.

A little river steamboat, the *Lizzie Horner,* was unloaded from Kennecott's ship at Saint Michael. However, an essential part had been left behind: *Lizzie's* smokestack. That missing piece had to be made from scrap metal before she could be fired up. *Lizzie* proved to be a fussy steamer, and she broke down at all the worst times. The crew moved very slowly up the Yukon River that fall. Kennecott hated the slowness and suspected that his crew was tampering with the steamboat. After the Yukon River froze over, *Lizzie* was useless and they left her behind.

After the crew left the boat, Robert Kennecott had to act quickly. First, he needed to hire Russian-speaking Alaskan guides. The Americans would now travel into Athabaskan country, where the only common language was Russian. This process was extremely frustrating for Kennecott because he found that while the natives were very willing to work, they wanted a whole dollar a day! As expedition chief, Kennecott hated to spend so much on common labor. He also disliked paying high wages to laborers while the scientists worked for much less. Likewise, buying sleds and dogs was a challenge since native mushers wanted big money. Kennecott's San Francisco men proved to be awful dog drivers, and as Kennecott eyed his diminishing store of supplies, he wondered how he would feed a bunch of husky dogs when he could barely feed his own men.

The harsh arctic winter came too quickly, and the temperature plummeted to thirty below zero. The wind howled as loud as the huskies. Even so, the camp managed to move up the Yukon River every few weeks. They were pleased to see that as they traveled upriver, they found more and larger trees than they had seen on the coast. Some men built crude huts to ward off the chilly wind. The midwinter sun shone for only a few hours a day, so the men worked primarily by moonlight. On moonless nights, they huddled around lanterns in their tents and huts. Meals had been reduced to biscuits at breakfast, and a dinner of salt meat with biscuits. It was hard to keep warm on only two meals a day. Kennecott feared that the men were cursing him and kept to himself. He became moody and depressed.

The spring of 1866 found the group camping at the dilapidated Russian fort of Nulato. Over the course of the fall and winter, they had managed to travel 550 miles up the Yukon River. On the morning of

May 13, Kennecott sat down and wrote guidelines for the expedition should he die. This note was placed where the crew was sure to find it. He then left the Nulato camp alone and strolled along the Yukon River. The river ice had broken, and the snow was patchy in the forest. Pausing at one point, he studied the landscape. The river twisted and braided around islands. Feeder creeks tumbled down the hillside. How would he map this? Where was true north? Taking a compass out of his pocket, he traced its symbols in the sand with a stick. Kennecott was finally doing what he most loved—collecting information about the natural world.

When Kennecott did not return for dinner, two crewmen went searching for him. They soon found his body on the bank of the river, with a peaceful look on his face. One of the men believed that Kennecott's heart had simply stopped. The other was sure that Kennecott had committed suicide, for hadn't he left a suicide note in his tent? There was no evidence to decide the matter for them, and the mystery of Kennecott's passing remains just that today.

Kennecott had been in Alaska less than nine months. Ironically, the most time he was able to spend with any of his scientists occurred when one of them escorted his coffin back to San Francisco.

It took three men to fill Kennecott's shoes. The twenty-year-old fish expert became chief of the Scientific Corps and continued the work of taking notes and collecting samples. Meanwhile, a company man pushed the Yukon River team to complete their exploration. With another expedition man and a guide, he paddled all the way up to the source of the Yukon in Canada, to mark the intended route for the line. The coastal crew chief led his men in exploration and trail brushing from the Yukon River to the Bering Strait.

The crews toiled another entire year, traveling slowly and digging into frozen ground. The coastal crew was the only Alaska team to erect telephone poles and then only along 80 miles of trail. Then came news. In the summer of 1867, the Russian American division learned that a telegraph wire had been laid across an ocean—the Atlantic Ocean. America and Europe were connected, but not by them. The Western Union Telegraph Company immediately decided it would spend no more money on a Bering Strait line, and the crew was fired. The men dropped their shovels and cheered for joy! There was a second piece of news as well: America had purchased Alaska from Russia.

Although the dream of a transpacific telegraph line had failed, the expedition was a scientific success. The Scientific Corps had collected a great volume of natural history information, and several expedition naturalists returned to the United States with samples and rough drafts of books. America quickly knew more about Interior Alaska than Russia ever had. All of this research took place because Robert Kennecott had insisted on bringing scientists along on his expedition to Alaska.

DID AMERICA BUY FORT YUKON?

- 1869 -

Fort Yukon

THE FOURTH OF JULY, 1869, WAS A GRAND DAY. An American flag waved from the flagpole in the town of Saint Michael, and "Alaska Commercial Company" (ACC) was newly painted on much of what was there. A large ACC ship was anchored in the Bering Sea, and an ACC river steamship, the *Yukon,* sat at the mouth of the Yukon River. With much celebration the little steamer left Saint Michael for its maiden voyage up the Yukon. The trading post agent gave them a hearty send-off, not knowing if he would ever see the ship again.

No steamship had ever traveled the 1,300 miles to Fort Yukon before. The ACC ship captain and crew were transporting ACC traders, American trappers, and three soldiers. Captain Charles Raymond, of the U.S. Army Corps of Engineers, was on a mission to solve the mystery of the Alaska-Canada border. Where was the border, and which side of it did Fort Yukon occupy? What, exactly, had the United States bought from the Russians in 1867?

Two years earlier, the United States had purchased Alaska from Russia for $7.2 million. Many called the purchase of this "icebox" a folly. Yet there were San Francisco businessmen who thought that Alaska could make them rich. Together, they formed the ACC, a trading conglomerate intent on filling the gap left by the departing Russian traders. The ACC purchased all of the buildings, ships, and trade goods that the Russian-American Company was unloading. Saint Michael's buildings were among their purchases. The steamship *Yukon* was part of the ACC's plan to place a string of fur traders along the Yukon River. Government land permits were easy for the ACC to get, as the U.S. was eager to see Alaska developed. The company hoped they could make Fort Yukon a major trading post, but they only cared to try if the fort was actually within the Alaskan border. The ACC was happy to see the three government men initiate this endeavor.

Captain Raymond had a second assignment from the government: he was to draw a map of the Yukon River and take notes on everything he saw. He constantly sketched islands, forks, and feeder creeks, labeling native villages and ACC trading posts on his map. He filled his notebook with questions. Could an American company make money logging here? What about trapping? Did the trappers find enough beaver and fox? Was farming possible in this northern land? Were the summers long enough and warm enough? What fish lived here? Were there enough to support a fishing industry?

The 50-foot *Yukon* huffed and puffed up the Yukon River. It was a stern-wheeler and had neither sails nor oars. Instead, a wood-burning furnace powered the motor that turned the great wheel, and each rotation of the waterwheel moved the ship upriver against the current. The boatmen worked hard to feed the furnace. The motor was extremely noisy and the smokestack belched smoke, which was acrid and annoying, but did serve to keep the mosquitoes away. The ship frequently had to stop onshore to take on more firewood. The trees were small and scarce near the coast, but became thicker and bigger as the boat powered up the river. Although the river was wide, it was also braided with many islands and sandbars. The crew had to select channels carefully, as it was easy to run aground. Dead trees reached up from the river bottom, snagging the Yukon's water-wheel. Furthermore, the map they had was so rough that it was almost useless. Fortunately for them the sun never set—they needed the assurance of the sunlight since they rarely knew what was around the next bend.

As the ship chugged up the river and into dark forestland, it eventually entered Athabaskan territory. The Athabaskans were totally amazed by the smoke-breathing monster. Captain Raymond's uniform was something new also. He was the first U.S. military man to travel up the Yukon. The Athabaskans had been trading with white men for a few years, but those white traders had always trav-eled, dressed, and lived much as the natives did. The ACC and U.S. Army men had a very different style, and the Athabaskans were not sure they liked it.

The Yukon River slices through the heart of Alaska, drawing water from a number of lesser rivers. The names of the rivers sound like music: Anvik, Koyukuk, and Tanana. Villages, lone cabins, and tiny trading posts sat at the mouths of many of these rivers, with the largest interior ACC post at the Tanana River. The steamship stopped at this trading post to drop off supplies and some of its passengers, primarily trappers and traders. It was the peak of the annual salmon run, and Raymond studiously jotted notes in his notebook as he watched the locals fishing. Fish were hung to dry on wooden frames, and Raymond noted that the Athabaskan diet appeared to be mostly salmon. As the boat continued up the river, days passed without any-one seeing a cabin or fish camp. However, plenty of wildlife came down to the riverbank, including moose, caribou, wolves, grizzly bears, and black bears.

The *Yukon* arrived in Fort Yukon, her final destination, at the end of July. Raymond and his crew had traveled an incredible 1,300 miles in less than a month. Fort Yukon was a trading post that was served by the Hudson's Bay Company. The managers of the Hudson's Bay Company knew that the fort might be in Alaska and not in Canada at all, but the Russians had never objected to their presence, so they all had just gone about their business. However, in 1868, rowdy American trappers threatened a Hudson's Bay Company agent, accusing the Canadian of buying furs within the border in Alaska. The Hudson's Bay Company office suspected that the Americans were correct about the location of the border and secretly sent word to their Fort Yukon agent telling him not to defend the fort. If the Americans demanded Fort Yukon, he was told to just give it to them.

Fort Yukon sat on a piece of high ground where the Porcupine River emptied into the Yukon. There were four guardhouses grouped around a few other buildings, all of which were made of log. Beyond the guardhouses, Raymond and two of his men set up two canvas wall tents, end-to-end. Two slits were cut in the roof, and below the roof openings, the men erected Raymond's zenith telescope and engineer's transit. They waved good-bye to the departing steamship, and then waited for a clear night to study the sky and compute the latitude and longitude.

For several days, the sky over Fort Yukon was cloudy. While he waited for the sky to clear, Raymond used the time to study the area. Could one farm in Fort Yukon? He dug a hole in the ground, and to his surprise, his shovel hit ice only two feet down. This was early August—farming did not look very promising. On these days with no real work to do, Raymond also spent a bit of time getting to know Fort Yukon's two Anglican missionaries. Raymond enjoyed hearing of their experiences and was impressed that the priests were so serious about bringing Christianity to the Athabaskans that they were learning the local dialect, Kutchin.

On August 7, 1869, there was a solar eclipse. While the moon passed in front of the sun, Raymond focused his telescope and transit. Now was the time to finally fulfill the primary purpose of his expedition. With his instruments lined up, he figured the latitude and longitude of Fort Yukon. The latitude was interesting: Fort Yukon sat on the Arctic Circle. However, the big news was the longitude. Fort Yukon was not on the Alaska-Canada border. It was 121 miles inside Alaska!

Captain Raymond told the news to the Hudson's Bay Company agent. While he saw no need to be rude, he did inform the Canadians that they were trespassing on American soil. Raymond formally took over the company's buildings in the name of the United States of America. The transition of rule between the two countries passed without incident. The company agent quietly packed up and went back to Canada, and the two missionaries left to do their preaching from the Canadian side of the border. His mission for the army completed, Raymond had no desire to spend the winter in Fort Yukon. He and his two soldiers decided to build a raft to float down the Yukon River. Their boat leaked so badly, however, that they had to stop often for repairs. They eventually abandoned it, and it was late September when they finally arrived at Saint Michael. Captain Raymond was eager to share the great news with the ACC agent. The Fort Yukon trading post was theirs to buy!

The Athabaskans cared little about this border settlement between the United States and Canada. And why should they have? There was no line on the ground, and they had been traveling between summer fish camps and winter trapping camps for centuries with no regard for imaginary lines.

Although the Alaskan landscape was wonderful, Charles Raymond was not so sure that Americans could get rich there. In his view, the Alaskan fur trade could grow no larger, and he saw little promise in farming, logging, or fishing. Despite his concerns, the ACC was counting on growing rich in Alaska.

Captain Raymond had finished his mission. He had proven that Fort Yukon was in Alaska, and he had drawn the first good map of the mighty Yukon River. And importantly, the United States finally knew exactly what it had bought.

ADVENTURE ON ICE

- 1880 -

Glacier Bay

A GREAT CANOE BOBBED IN WRANGELL HARBOR, fully loaded with camping supplies. It was early August in 1880, and John Muir's eyes crackled with impatience. He was beyond ready to start his trip, but instead there he sat, waiting. Finally, Reverend Samuel Hall Young came running down the dock, with his dog behind him. After climbing into the canoe, Young called to the dog, Stickeen, and the small, black mutt leaped into the canoe and snuggled up in Young's coat.

Muir protested, saying the dog was too small to be useful and would only cause trouble, but Young refused to leave Stickeen behind. Though small, the dog was good company. The two-year-old Sheltie-mix had been a wedding present to Young and his wife, who were Wrangell's Presbyterian missionaries. The Wrangell natives, Stickeen Tlingits, had named the dog. John Muir wanted to set off more than he wanted to argue, but he privately wondered if the dog would survive the trip.

The cedar canoe was piloted by a Wrangell guide, Lot Tyeen, who had brought with him his son-in-law, Joe, an excellent hunter and cook. Seventeen-year-old Billy, a local boy, was coming because he spoke both good English and Tlingit. Once the decision was made about bringing the dog, the five men were ready to set out.

Naturalist John Muir was not the first tourist to come to the Alaska Panhandle, but he may have been the most famous early one. His writings had appeared in American magazines and he was known across the United States. On his first Alaskan trip the previous summer, he had met Reverend Young and they had instantly become friends. The missionary admired the naturalist's enthusiasm and stamina and asked him to stay on in Wrangell as his houseguest. Muir, in turn, talked his new friend into sharing a lengthy paddle trip that fall. The two and their guides had reached Glacier Bay before needing to return to Wrangell so Muir could make the last steamer home. Muir hadn't had nearly enough time there, and was eager to explore Glacier Bay again and take more notes. By studying Alaska's vibrant glaciers, he hoped to better understand California's small ones. This 1880 journey was a tourist trip with a serious mission.

For a map, Muir had a copy of one that had been made seventy years earlier. The coastline was drawn poorly, with few bays and glaciers marked. As they traveled, Muir corrected the lines of the map and gave names to many landmarks.

Wrangell lies halfway down the Alaska Panhandle, and Glacier Bay is more than 200 miles to its north. The group paddled the dugout canoe north through the many islands. Muir was in a hurry to see glaciers, lots of glaciers! He pushed the men to paddle for long days. Along the way they explored narrow, glacier-carved bays called fjords. This amused the guides. Why explore a bay, so icy that there was no hope of finding gold or game? Lot tied tree branches to the outer edge of his canoe to protect it from floating ice, and the men used long sticks to push away icebergs. Chunks of dense, blue ice crashed down from the steep ice walls, sending great waves across the bay. The native men were uncomfortable exploring so dangerously close to the ice. If they fell in, they would quickly die. Nonetheless, Muir had plotted a course and he planned to stick to it. He knew the season was short and they had to move quickly if he was going to make much progress with his map and notes.

When the party finally stopped to camp each night, Muir eagerly explored the land. Stickeen, the dog, followed him on all of his hikes. After a week, Muir admitted that he liked the dog, and the feeling was clearly mutual. Envious of their forays, Reverend Young usually stayed behind in camp since he suffered from a bad shoulder that prevented him from rock climbing.

In three weeks, the canoe reached Glacier Bay, a huge gash carved by numerous glaciers that poured down from either side. The group explored 60 miles deep into the iceberg-filled bay, stopping for a full week at grand Muir Glacier. Muir had seen and named this glacier on his 1879 trip, and it again filled him with awe.

After leaving Glacier Bay, they paddled west, coming to a smaller bay that was not on the map (now known as Taylor Bay). The sky was thick with fog, and rain drizzled on the men, soaking them to the skin. It took all of their strength to paddle to shore through the icebergs. On shore, they set up camp by a glacier. Muir was fascinated with this glacier: it appeared to be growing, while the others were getting smaller. Muir couldn't figure out why, and he soon declared to Young that he would spend the next day exploring the glacier, which he called Taylor Glacier.

Muir rose early and took no time for breakfast. A storm was brewing and he was in a hurry. Muir's Scottish soul loved the drama of adverse weather, and he was particularly eager to experience this glacier in a snowstorm. If the new snow fed the glacier's growth, he wanted to witness it. He dropped a biscuit in his pocket and picked up his ice axe. Stickeen insisted on joining him, though Muir told the dog to stay. Soon the two were climbing up on the ice. The sky broke for a few minutes, giving Muir a longer look at the extensive glacier, which he estimated to be 8 miles wide at the water's edge. He quickly took out his notebook and drew it. The glacier was like a river of ice flowing down the mountainside, and like a flooded river, the glacier was overflowing its banks. It was uprooting trees on either side, and rocks, even great boulders, were tossed aside. It was carving the valley, just as it had carved the bay. The pressure of movement ripped the ice into great cracks called crevasses. Nature was giving him a science lesson, and Muir was a willing student.

Muir used his axe to cut steps into steep rises so that the little dog could follow him. Together, they hiked along the east bank of the glacier. This was easy enough, so he crossed the width of the glacier. The glacier center was flowing faster than the sides and was buckling into great crevasses. He figured some of these crevasses were 1,000 feet deep and 30 feet across. Leaping over cracks as wide as 8 feet, Muir was impressed to see the little dog follow. On the glacier's west bank, they hiked upward again. Finally, he came to an awesome lake filled with bobbing icebergs. It was beautiful, but it was getting late and was time to leave.

Muir headed down, taking what he thought was the shortest route. By this time the snow was blowing harder and he wandered blindly into a maze of cracks. Muir was getting a bit nervous and wasn't entirely sure how he would get back. He had to keep his eyes trained down so he wouldn't fall into a crevasse, which concerned him since he couldn't plan a route carefully if he was always watching his feet. Nonetheless, he kept going in what he thought was the right direction, leaping over crevasses when he came to them. Stickeen leaped too. Eventually, however, the crevasses got wider, until they could not be jumped. Muir kept hoping each large crevasse would be the last. The snow was thick, night was coming, and Muir began to suspect that he would have to spend the night on the glacier.

Man and dog came to one crevasse that was much longer and wider than the others. Unable to bear the idea of trying to walk around it, Muir finally found a place where he dared to leap. Luckily, he reached the other side without sliding back into the depths. Stickeen flew across also. But the very next step posed a huge challenge. Muir was standing on an ice island. The only way off was an ice bridge that would require Muir to climb several feet down the wall of his island, leaving him suspended in air hundreds of feet above a certain and icy death. Cutting steps with his axe, he carefully crawled down the ice bridge. As he slid along the bridge on his stomach, he flattened it with the axe. Once on the other side, Muir called for Stickeen, but the dog cried and refused to follow. Muir was amazed that the dog understood the greater danger present. After much begging from Muir, the dog stepped slowly down the ice steps to the ice bridge. Any slip would have sent him tumbling to his death. Treading slowly and whining the whole time, Stickeen finally made it to Muir. Safe! The rest of the journey down the glacier was so easy that they almost skipped with joy.

It was late when Muir and Stickeen returned to camp. They had been gone seventeen hours and were miserably cold and hungry. Muir immediately changed into dry clothes and ate a bowl of hot chowder. Once full, he told Reverend Young about their adventure and heaped praise on Stickeen.

Reverend Young had a story to tell also. The camp had had guests, a Hoonah Tlingit chief and the man's three wives. The visitors gave Young gifts of porpoise meat, salmon, clams, crabs, and strawberries. Young was amazed to see strawberries growing this far north.

Then, the visitor asked a favor. Could Reverend Young pray to his god to stop the glacier from advancing? It was blocking off a valuable salmon stream and in a few years it would totally cover the stream. Hoping to please the glacier spirit, the chief had already killed two of his slaves. The missionary saw this story as proof that these people needed Christianity. Muir saw it as proof that the glacier was growing. Further studies would confirm to Muir that he was correct in theorizing that snow accumulation fed the glaciers, and that increased precipitation would push a glacier downhill. Later scientists would establish that a steep rock bed under the glacier hastens its movement.

From Taylor Bay the group quickly paddled south. Muir was in a hurry to catch the southbound September mail ship. His canoe trip had lasted about six weeks, and he needed to return home to California.

Muir shared his map with the United States government since it was much better than any other map available at the time. Using his notes from the summer's trip, he also wrote magazine articles and books. Stickeen, the story of Alaska's brave ice-climbing dog, touched America and became his best-loved book. Glacier Bay National Park includes the glacier of Stickeen's adventure, now known as Brady Glacier.

COOK INLET SHIPWRECK

- 1890 -

Cook Inlet

ON APRIL 23, 1890, THE *Corea,* an old-fashioned, tall, three-masted sailing ship, was finishing a long journey from San Francisco to Alaska's Cook Inlet. The sailors had been looking forward to this day for a long time, but things were not turning out quite as they had expected. The inlet was stormy and the ship was fighting a strong tide. Without a steam engine, the *Corea* was at the mercy of the wind, and the wind was showing no mercy. It was three in the morning and still quite dark, but none of the 116 men aboard wanted to drop sail and wait until sunrise to try again. Their destination was just around the corner. Hold that rudder! Fight that wind! Stay away from the coast!

Despite their best efforts, the men were unable to fight the winds blowing them to shore. The *Corea* rammed hard into a sandbar. She was stuck tight 20 miles from her destination, the Kasilof River fish cannery. The wind rocked her from side to side, but it was not enough to free her from the sand. As the men debated their options, they noticed that the tide was beginning to go out. They had no idea how they were going to free the ship, but they could see that the tide wasn't going to help them—and no one else would be able to do so either. The *Corea* was the largest ship serving Cook Inlet; there would be no other ship powerful enough to pull them out.

As the sun rose over the mountain and night turned to morning, the men studied the area marked on their map as the Kenai Peninsula. They were close to shore, and the retreating tide left a wide, rocky beach where enormous black rocks were scattered. Bushes and small trees grew beyond the high-tide line, and a creek burbled through the snow-covered ground. The land near them was hilly, but not mountainous. However, they could see mountains, huge ones, on the far side of Cook Inlet. All in all, it was a gorgeous place to be stuck.

The *Corea* had two longboats, and a few of the old cannery hands were eager to row to the Kasilof cannery for help. It would take just a few hours, and they knew that a winter watchman would be there. More importantly, there were fishing boats stored at the cannery, and perhaps those boats could be used to help tug the Corea off the sandbar. After the winds died down, the longboats were lowered and rowed north along the coast to Kasilof.

Two days later, the fishing boats finally arrived back from Kasilof. The men knew they would have to lighten the *Corea*'s load to have any hope of pulling her free of the sand. No one wanted to think about the fact that even when she was empty, the ship still weighted a hefty 565 tons. Before they could begin the work of pulling the boat off the sandbar, the men set to work hauling supplies off the ship. There was $95,000 worth of summer supplies on board, including flat salmon cans, food for the mess hall, supplies for the dormitory, and stock for the company store. There were also odd tools, machinery, and building materials. Boxes and sacks were slowly lowered to much smaller fishing boats, to be hauled to Kasilof.

The cannery buildings and dock at the mouth of the Kasilof River were owned by the Alaska Packing Company. The San Francisco-based firm had started the cannery only eight years earlier, in 1882. This was the first cannery on Cook Inlet, and only the second cannery in all of Alaska. Business was brisk for the Alaska Packing Company since America was quickly learning to enjoy canned Alaska red salmon. Good cooks preferred it to the salted Alaska salmon that had been available for two decades.

The Alaska Packing Company's *Corea* was named for the Asian kingdom of Korea. Under its first owner, it was a trading vessel that sailed between California and Asia. The *Corea* was the first large cannery ship to serve Cook Inlet. Starting in 1885, it arrived every April with workers and supplies, returning to San Francisco with canned red salmon and laid-off workers. The cannery was typically closed down by early September, with only the winter watchman left. If the *Corea* was not freed, how would the Alaska Packing Company get its Cook Inlet fish to market?

In early April, the crew of the *Corea* had boarded the ship in San Francisco, tempted by the Alaska Packing Company's offer of summer work. They could have just as easily boarded the company's other ship and traveled to its other Alaska cannery. In fact, there were several companies in San Francisco that were hiring cannery workers. Most of these had "Alaska" in their name, but the company offices and owners were in California. Similarly, the profits did not stay in Alaska. The new process of canning made it possible to sell fish caught in Alaskan waters to customers thousands of miles away, and San Francisco businessmen were sure they could get rich from this enterprise.

While unloading the ship was easy enough, freeing it from the sandbar proved impossible. No matter how many little boats tried, they could not move the huge ship. In fact, tides came and left twice a day, adding more sand to the sandbar, burying the *Corea* even deeper. The men were at a loss. They had no idea if the company could get another ship to Cook Inlet this summer. What should the Kasilof crew do in the meantime? If there was no way to get the fish back to San Francisco, why bother to catch or can any?

In the end, the Alaska Packing Company's Kasilof cannery did not operate during the summer of 1890. In a good summer the cannery shipped 40,000 cases of canned salmon south; this year they sent none. The *Corea* was left in the sandbar to fall apart. Eventually, the cannery workers found other transportation back to San Francisco. One Finnish man decided he liked the Kenai Peninsula and stayed. He joined a growing number of cannery workers who were building cabins along the Kasilof and Kenai rivers.

In April 1891, a new Alaska Packing Company ship arrived in Cook Inlet. It had new workers and supplies for the Kasilof cannery. That summer it was one of thirty-five canneries processing fish in Alaska. The canneries made a lot of money for companies in San Francisco, Seattle, and Portland. Shipwrecks were part of the cost of doing business, and while the loss of the *Corea* was irksome for the company, it wasn't an unexpected blow. The profits were large enough that if a cannery burned down or was damaged by an avalanche, it could be rebuilt.

Winter ice eventually crushed the wooden hull of the *Corea*. Even though the great ship was gone, it was not forgotten, and the industrious people of Cook Inlet found many ways to use what they could salvage. Wood from the wreck was used in fish traps, cabins, and boats. The *Corea's* load of flat fish cans was used to side the Alaska Packing Company's winter watchman's house in Kasilof. In addition, a creek near the *Corea* wreck site was named Corea Creek. The final resting site of the *Corea* is still marked on many maps, and today's visitors can gaze out across the inlet and envision the grand, three-masted lady.

POWERFUL GIVING

- 1890 -

Klukwan

IN MARCH 1890, THE CHILKAT TLINGITS HAD A GREAT potlatch in honor of two young female members of the tribe. Not only was this a celebration, it was an act of defiance. The U.S. government had outlawed potlatches in 1884, because missionaries claimed they were wasteful and pagan. The Tlingits ran the risk of having their ceremonial items seized by government officials, yet they resisted giving up this long-held tradition.

A potlatch was one of the most important ceremonial events in the Tlingit culture, one that helped knit together the villages, clans, and houses. Potlatches were held for a variety of important occasions, including funerals, the building of a clan house, or the raising of a totem pole. It was a time for the hosts to give away much of their wealth, with the knowledge that the guest would repay the debt in the future. In fact, the word potlatch means "give away." In the spring of 1890, the potlatch to honor the coming of age of two teenagers was also a way for the Tlingits to reinforce their family structure which was constantly being undermined by missionaries and canneries.

The potlatch was to be held at an old Chilkat Tlingit village, Yen-da-Stucka, which had large, traditional, multi-family clan houses, plus smaller single-family homes in the style of white people. Because the Ravens were the hosts, the event would take place at the Raven House. The Eagles were their guests. The two groups were related by marriage, as tradition dictated that Ravens could only marry Eagles.

Chief George Shotridge, a Raven, was married to an Eagle woman. In this matrilineal society, this meant that their four children were also Eagles. In order to celebrate the coming-of-age of a Shotridge daughter and a niece, Eagle guests were invited from Tlingit villages as far away as 200 miles. The Ravens wanted to prove they were a rich and generous people: wealth equaled power, but only if one gave it away.

In preparation for the potlatch, the chief's men had cut wood for the local cannery. The new cannery caretaker, a twenty-four-year-old white man named Ben Moore, wanted 370 cords—a stack the size of a large house—in reserve for the cannery's next summer operation. For the wood, Chief Shotridge was paid $550 in cannery store tickets, and all of this credit was spent on gifts for the potlatch. In the company store, Shotridge selected numerous brown-wool blankets, then filled out his order with bolts of printed cotton fabric, tobacco, sugar, crackers, flour, and clothing. Ben Moore wrote the purchases in the store ledger, while the Raven men carried the goods out the door. Traditionally, the essential potlatch gift had been a hand-woven blanket; however, times were changing and trading post goods were replacing more labor-intensive, handmade items.

On the first morning of the potlatch, many of the guests crammed into the Raven House. In years past, this building would have been the home of twenty-five Ravens, but now it was used as their ceremonial hall. The space was packed with over 500 men, women, and children, all anticipating the gifts they would soon receive. The house wouldn't hold everyone, and many people milled around outside, wishing they could join in. The fact that there were no windows and only an overhead smoke hole to let in light added to the intense communal feeling.

Chief Shotridge, a muscular 6-foot man, stood on the stage, and the room quieted. Like other Chilkat men, Shotridge wore his hair short and had a mustache. Behind him was a great wooden screen painted with images of fierce animals. Each animal was vibrantly colored and had huge eyes and very large mouths. The stage was set with large bentwood boxes, which stored the special clothes, drums, bowls, and other necessary supplies.

Two pretty, teenage girls shyly looked out from behind the stage screen. Shotridge's daughter, Klinget-sai-yet, was a fine-boned beauty of fifteen with long, black hair. She and her cousin, having reached puberty, had been hidden from the community for many months. During that time, Klinget-sai-yet's mother and her aunt had taught the girls to be traditional Tlingit wives. They learned poise and good manners, plus housekeeping and craft skills. For Klinget-sai-yet, a high-ranking Eagle, a proper traditional marriage would be to a high-ranking Raven. Yet the world of the Tlingit was rapidly changing. Chief Shotridge was attempting to be true to his Tlingit values while adopting a few white American ways.

Chief Shotridge slashed the binding cord on a bale of blankets. Then he cut the first blanket into 6-inch strips. Why? To prove that he was so rich that he cared nothing for material goods. In a booming voice, Shotridge named the guests who were to receive each strip.

This same process was repeated again and again, and yet at the end of the first day, there were still blankets to distribute. Everyone knew that each guest would receive many blanket strips. Once home, the guests would sew the strips together into patchwork blankets that would become a treasured reminder of the great potlatch.

On the second day, Chief Shotridge began distributing the fabric, food, and clothing. These were handed out in the same way, with a few yards of fabric being given to many guests. Gift giving would go on for yet another day. By giving so generously, Chief Shotridge impressed his Eagle guests; of equal importance, his fellow Ravens were proud of his generosity and would permit him to continue as their chief.

While gift giving continued all day, the evening was for dancing. The female dancers had painted faces and wore earrings and nose rings. From their shoulders hung beautiful, blue-black button blankets that were trimmed with red borders. Patterns of ravens and eagles were worked out in hundreds of white pearl buttons, resulting in elaborate and beautiful designs. The men had painted faces also. They wore beaded jackets, aprons, leggings, and moccasins. Many of these garments were made from blankets woven of mountain goat wool, which had been received at past potlatches. Some men did not wear vests, but had fully painted chests instead. On their heads, they wore raven or eagle heads and wings.

Drums and raven-shaped rattles kept the rhythm of the dance. The women stood in a line on the stage, swaying back and forth and singing like ravens and eagles. The men were lined up below the platform, where they jumped around like angry birds. One strong, young Eagle man jumped over the heads of the other dancers. As the dancing grew more and more frenzied, the room became hotter and hotter. Long ago someone had carved a 12-foot-long, flat stick, which had long black human hair attached to the end. The stick was held over favorite dancers, and when draped in this veil, the talented Eagle dancer danced even harder. He was in a contest, where each clan tried to prove they were the better dancers. Dancing went on for half the night, until everyone was exhausted. Some people stayed in the great house to talk until they dozed off, while others left to sleep in smaller village homes. Each homeowner invited guests to join them for the night.

Eventually, Chief Shotridge's family of six left for their private home. Shotridge invited a guest, Ben Moore, to their two-room home. Shotridge's wife prepared dinner, while Moore chatted with the chief. After the food was placed on the table, the chief's two daughters were summoned, and Klinget-sai-yet and her cousin emerged. Being well-bred girls, they stayed silent unless spoken to and kept their eyes cast down. After the chief introduced them, everyone ate. Shotridge insisted that the guest eat his fill, and then they shared cigars before turning in for the night. Moore was given the main room for himself, while the entire Shotridge family slept in the other room.

After the distribution of the last gifts on the third day, more dancing ensued. When the potlatch was finally over, the Eagle guests piled their canoes high with blanket strips, clothing, and food for the journey home. They left, knowing they would have to invite the Ravens to an Eagle potlatch, and that their potlatch would have to be at least as generous as the Ravens' had been.

Ben Moore continued to visit the Shotridge family that winter. Chief Shotridge was impressed with the young man's position managing the cannery's property and goods, a role not unlike that of a chief's. Furthermore, he possessed the valuable skills of reading, writing, and arithmetic. Unbeknownst to Moore, he was being regarded as an acceptable suitor for Klinget-sai-yet. He needed little nudging, as he was smitten by the girl's beauty and sweetness, and had started calling her "Minnie." Only six months after the potlatch, Ben married Minnie in a traditional Tlingit ceremony. Shortly thereafter, they confirmed their marriage in a Presbyterian ceremony. Initially, Ben met his wife's family expectations of generosity, but once he became wealthy and gained stature in the white community, he ceased to fill his obligations to his in-laws. Minnie's regal poise and stunning good looks served her well in formal white society, but her Tlingit silence hid her inner sadness for lost traditions. Ben and Minnie had three children, all Eagles, who rarely visited the traditional land of the Chilkat Tlingit and never hosted a potlatch. Eventually, the village of Yen-da-Stucka fell to ruins.

REINDEER RESCUE

- 1894 -

Teller

IN LATE JULY 1894, A WHALING SHIP CRUISED the Bering Sea. Oddly, it appeared to be carrying a load of Santa's helpers. At the railing was a line of passengers dressed in red and blue. All had fair skin and hair, and the men had beards. Their long garments were embroidered with flowers and animals, and the toes of their boots curled up. Several sleighs were tied on the deck, and nearly a dozen dogs scrambled about. These mysterious visitors had their eyes trained on the Seward Peninsula, where tundra extended as far as the eye could see and pools of water shone like jewels. Realizing they were close to the Arctic Circle, the members of this village-at-sea took stock of the land they were to live on for at least the next three years. They were not surprised to see that it looked much like the home they had left behind.

William Kjellmann was in charge of the expedition. He and his companions had traveled from Norway by ship and train for the past fifteen weeks. Several months before that, he had answered a newspaper ad seeking, to his surprise and delight, a Laplander to lead the Alaska Reindeer Project. Laplanders, or Sami, are nomads of northern Scandinavia. Kjellmann, at age thirty-two, knew he was perfect for the job. He had lived in America for a few years, in the heartland state of Wisconsin, so he knew English and was familiar with how to arrange travel in America. More importantly, although he was Norwegian, he had been a reindeer herder and meat buyer in Lapland. In addition, he spoke Lapp as well as Norwegian. His letter to the project organizer stood out over those of the 250 other hopeful applicants, and he was quickly hired. Kjellmann soon set out on the recruiting trip to northern Norway, and while there he found exactly the people he was looking for: six couples with four children among them, plus a single man. All were reindeer herders willing to sign three-year contracts of service in Alaska. They were also Christians, as required by the project organizer, an American minister. They were promised housing, food, pay (or reindeer), and equal rights (something that the Laplanders did not have in Norway). On the train trip across America, Kjellmann's father, wife, two daughters, and a Lutheran missionary family joined the party.

Second-in-command was Reverend Tollef Brevig. A Norwegian by birth, he had also lived in America, specifically Minnesota, for several years. He was pleased to know that the project organizer required a minister and that the Laplanders had specified that he be Lutheran. His wife and baby boy were by his side. Brevig looked forward to spreading Christianity to Native Alaskans.

This expedition was the special project of Dr. Sheldon Jackson, who was both a Presbyterian missionary and the U.S. General Agent of Education in Alaska. The Alaska Reindeer Project was Jackson's grand scheme to end famine in the territory. He was keenly aware that whaling ships were killing great numbers of sea mammals and caribou, leaving the natives without enough to eat. A few winters earlier, more than 1,000 Eskimos had starved to death on a single Alaska island. Jackson knew that some Siberians herded reindeer and never suffered famine. He surmised that teaching Alaskan Eskimos to herd reindeer was the solution to ending their famine.

As the ship arrived, the Laplanders saw two white canvas tents on the beach. Behind them were driftwood pens for the reindeer and rough shacks that served as storage buildings. Nearly 200 reindeer looked up from the tundra. This was Teller Reindeer Station, named after a U.S. congressman who believed in Jackson's project. Dr. Jackson had set up the station the summer before and stocked it with 175 Siberian reindeer. The station needed work, but the Laplanders were eager to give it a try.

It took some time to unload the ship, but everyone was glad to walk on land again. Life at the station soon settled into a pleasant, busy rhythm. The Laplanders made tipi-frames for their reindeer-skin tents, just as they had done at home. When not helping their parents set up camp, the children picked berries and tried catching fish. The Kjellmann girls learned camping skills from the other children. On August 1, Reverend Brevig gave his first sermon and the group gave thanks for their new home.

The local Inupiats visited Teller Reindeer Station and quickly warmed up to the Laplanders. They called the Laplanders "Card People" because of the men's four-cornered hats. The Inupiats liked the fact that the Laplanders came as families, and soon Inupiat and Lapp children were playing happily together. The young Laplanders taught them to play "Lapp ball" and ski, while the adults introduced turnips, rutabagas, and other root vegetables to the people of western Alaska. The two groups also traded fish-drying methods. Eventually, the Inupiats copied some of the bright colors and patterns of the Lapp clothing, and the Laplanders learned how to mush sled teams of huskies. The newcomers began breeding huskies in addition to their Lapp herding dogs.

The Laplanders believed, as the Inupiats did, that the plants and animals had spirits. One had to please the spirits and travel gently on the earth. When a person took something from nature, he had to give something back. Lapp life and values fit well with that of the locals.

For the Lapps, life rotated around the reindeer. They followed the animals from grazing place to grazing place, living in tents. The reindeer supplied them with meat, milk, cheese, and even glue. However, the animals were not only useful as food. Rope, fish lines, boots, snowshoes, blankets, and tents were made from the fur and skins; the horns and bones became needles, spoons, combs, handles, and sled runners. Furthermore, each reindeer could pull a load of 300 pounds and run for up to 50 miles. It wasn't uncommon to see a Lapp man lasso a reindeer and harness it to a sleigh, then ride grandly around the tundra, with his red and blue sashes flying in the wind.

One of the first Inupiats to be a project student was Anisarlook. As promised, he received a female reindeer and calf each year during his first five years of training, the completion of which qualified him to received a herd of 115 for himself. Anisarlook's success was proof of the project's value, and it motivated others to earn their own herds.

As word of the reindeer project spread, Eskimos from all over western Alaska applied to be a part of it. Sheldon Jackson included natives from as many villages as possible. It had been his hope that the Eskimos would switch from being hunter-gatherers to herders. To Jackson, and many other white Americans at the time, this would make them more "civilized."

Over the next ten years, the U.S. government spent over $200,000 on the project. More than 1,600 new reindeer and a hundred Lapp families were brought to Alaska. Some Laplanders took all of their pay in reindeer. About 40% of the reindeer were given to

Eskimos. Small herds were also moved from Teller to nine mission schools, and some reindeer were also left on several Aleutian Islands.

In 1898, a reindeer project man found gold on the Seward Peninsula, and the discovery started the Nome gold rush. By this time, William Kjellmann had led the Alaska Reindeer Project for five years. He added a new challenge to his life by staking gold claims in the Nome area. When he left Alaska to return to Wisconsin, he was gold rich. However, most of the Laplanders stayed behind. The Brevigs decided they loved Alaska. They soon had a second child and built a mission school near Teller, where they served the local Inupiats.

The reindeer project succeeded, and reindeer herds thrived in western Alaska. However, the project alone cannot be credited with bringing an end to hunger in Alaska. The whaling industry was fading into history, and as the whalers sailed away, the sea mammals were left in relative peace to live and procreate, as well as to once more provide food for local populations.

DEATH ON THE GLACIER

- 1897 -

Portage

IN THE SUMMER OF 1897, GEORGE HALL CAME to Alaska on a mission. He was looking for his friend, Charles Blackstone. Hall had made a promise to Blackstone's wife to find his friend, dead or alive.

Charles Blackstone had come down with "gold fever" the year before, and eventually his dreams of striking it rich in Alaska were too much to resist. Leaving his wife and children at home in Seattle, Blackstone headed north, fully expecting to return home a rich man. He asked his friend, George Hall, to watch after his family if he failed to return in the fall.

In late April 1896, Blackstone, along with 250 other men, climbed aboard a steamship bound for Alaska. He quickly befriended two other passengers, Charles Botcher and J. W. Malinque, who, like many on board, had never mined before. In place of experience, they each had camping supplies, shovels, picks, gold pans, and dreams.

They talked about gold—dust, flakes, and nuggets. The summer before, pounds of it had been found in a creek that fed Cook Inlet's Turnagain Arm. Everyone on the ship was sure that he would soon be rich too.

The ship arrived in Cook Inlet in early May, when the area was still in the grip of winter. The inlet was thick with chunks of ice, and the captain refused to travel up to Turnagain Arm. Instead, he anchored near the mouth of the inlet, some 200 miles from the gold streams. His crew would row the passengers ashore in longboats, but this was the end of the line for the ship. On the beach, there was still thick snow, but even so there was already one mining party camping there. These miners told the newcomers how hard it could be to travel in this wild country, and warned them that although the melting snow was a hassle, it wouldn't get much easier after the snow was gone. The Kenai Peninsula was a rainforest, and it was crisscrossed with streams, swamps, glaciers, and mountains. Walking through this maze was difficult at best. Boating up the inlet was not much easier. Some days the water shot through Turnagain Arm like a 30-foot wave; the miners weren't kidding when they called this tide the "cannonball," as it shot back any boat that tried to muscle past it.

While on Turnagain Arm, the men explored the main mining camps, optimistically called Hope City and Sunrise City. A trading post was being set up in each new location, giving the camps a stamp of respectability. The men were somewhat puzzled that there were large native villages elsewhere on Cook Inlet, but not on Turnagain Arm. It would be some time before they figured out that the Athabaskans knew Turnagain Arm had the worst boating on the inlet.

Mulling over all this information, the newcomers weighed their options. They had to decide quickly what they were going to do, since the captain was readying the ship to return to Seattle for another load of miners. Did anyone want to leave Alaska yet? Blackstone, Botcher, and Malinque, along with the majority of the other men, said no. Although things looked rough, they were not quitting. The second question was easier to answer: did anyone want to send a letter back to Seattle? There might not be another chance to send a letter home, so many of the men quickly jotted down their news and well wishes to their loved ones.

Other ships arrived in Cook Inlet and the tent camp at the inlet's mouth kept growing. Men were restless to get to the Turnagain Arm gold. Some cut down trees, sawed boards, and built crude boats and hand-carved oars. Hundreds hoped to row the 200 or so miles around the inlet.

One day, Botcher and a few others crept away from the camp and into the woods. They followed a river deep into the center of the Kenai Peninsula. There, they dipped their gold pans into creeks and swirled them until only the heaviest sand and a few gold flakes lay in the bottom. Flakes! One could not get rich working for a few flakes! Botcher had counted on gold nuggets and was sorely disappointed. The summer was passing fast and things did not look promising.

Rumors were flying up and down Cook Inlet. There were stories of $50 gold pans. There was also news of empty rowboats and bodies washed ashore. One unhappy miner wrote this little poem on a scrap of paper:

> *In God we trusted,*
> *In Alaska we busted,*
> *Let her rattle:*
> *Will try it again in old Seattle.*

Blackstone, Botcher, and Malinque gave up on Cook Inlet. In late summer, they left to look for gold up on the Yukon River. News of the Circle gold field was enticing, but they had missed the last Yukon River steamship of the season, and the 1,000-mile hike proved too much for the three. Discouraged, they were back on Turnagain Arm in March, poorer than they had been when they left.

Of the 3,000 gold miners on Turnagain Arm over the summer, there were only 300 left, including the 150 men wintering at Sunrise City. A year earlier, the camp had not even been a trading post, but in 1897 the boomtown had several stores, a brewery, two saloons, and two restaurants. Despite the comforts, the three men did not want to stay. Their funds were greatly depleted, their spirits were low, and they were tired of Alaska. Blackstone knew that his family would be worried about him.

Getting back to Seattle would not be easy, since no ships came to Sunrise City in the winter. Turnagain Arm was a ship captain's nightmare in winter: it was shallow, which meant that it froze, broke up, and froze again with each tide. On the other hand, deep Prince William Sound flowed all winter. To obtain winter passage on a ship, one had to hike to the sound.

The men of Sunrise City provided instructions on how to hike to Prince William Sound, as many of them had made the trip themselves. They also warned Botcher and his friends to watch out for fog and blizzards—both were common and could be deadly. They would also have to watch for great cracks in the ice, large enough to swallow a man forever. When they reached Portage Glacier, they were to follow the trail marked with stakes and ropes. If the men stayed on the marked trail, they should make it safely to the trading post at Portage Bay, where they could wait for the next ship south.

In Sunrise City, the Blackstone party packed with care. Their dog, Spot, was tied to a sled, which was piled high with food and blankets and covered with a moose hide. Ladders were lashed to the side and would serve as bridges if they needed to cross a wide crack in the ice. The men offered to carry letters to Seattle. A few letters, hoarded for months, were added to the load. On the morning of March 25, the three men left Sunrise City. Spot pulled the sled, while one man pulled its gee pole and another pushed from behind. Two days later, two men traveling to Sunrise saw the Blackstone party on Portage Glacier. Soon after this, however, a blizzard rose up, and Blackstone's group never reached the Portage Bay trading post.

Back in Seattle, Blackstone's wife feared the worst. George Hall took it upon himself to travel to Cook Inlet to find out what had happened. People in Sunrise City told him they remembered his friend, and directed Hall to follow the trail to Portage Glacier. He spent a fair amount of time on the glacier, searching for clues, footprints, and lost gear. Most of the footprints followed the rope trail, but not all. A few went off to the right, and Hall followed these. They went on and on, eventually wandering off of Portage Glacier. Not sure where to search next, he followed a mountain ridge for a long time, and then dropped down on a new glacier. Under a ledge of ice, he found the body of his friend, Charles Blackstone. Poor Charles's face and hands were black with frostbite. Pinned to his chest was this handwritten note:

Saturday, April 4th, 1897—This is to certify that Botcher froze to death on Tuesday night. J. W. Malinque died on Wednesday forenoon, being frozen so badly. C.A. Blackstone had his ears, nose, and four fingers on his right hand and two on his left hand frozen an inch back. The storm drove us on before it. It overtook us within an hour of the summit and drove us before it. It drove everything we had over the cliff except blankets and moose hide, which we all crawled

under. Supposed to have been forty degrees below zero.
On Friday I started for Salt Water. I don't know how I
got there. Have enough grub for ten days, providing
bad weather does not set in. Spot was blown over the
cliff. I think I can hear him howl once in awhile.

While unimaginable luck had brought Hall to Blackstone's body, he was not able to find the bodies of Botcher and Malinque, nor did anyone else report finding them. Hall sent a letter to Mrs. Blackstone reporting on his sorry discovery, and the story appeared in the Seattle newspaper that summer. Ironically, Hall had been bitten by gold fever and decided to stay on in Cook Inlet. That fall, he staked his own Turnagain Arm gold claim. Unfortunately, his creek was not very productive.

The Prince William Sound glacier where George Hall found his friend's body was named Blackstone Glacier. It feeds Blackstone Bay, where the shore is usually wrapped in fog or blowing snow. The wind still howls like a forsaken dog.

AVALANCHE ON THE CHILKOOT TRAIL

- 1898 -

Dyea

IN THE SUMMER OF 1897, HOARDS OF WOULD-BE MINERS stepped off ships in the Alaskan sister ports of Dyea and Skagway. While most thought that the hard part of the journey was over, they were in for a rude awakening. Six hundred long, hard miles separated the docks from the Klondike gold field. To tackle those 600 miles, newcomers had to choose between the trail in Dyea (known as the Chilkoot Trail) and the Skagway Trail. The 33-mile Chilkoot Trail was 8 miles shorter, but it was also much steeper. While the promoters of the Skagway Trail, a toll road, claimed it was a wagon trail, no such claim was made of the Chilkoot, because the Chilkoot Pass was much too steep for a horse to scale. The Chilkoot was called the "poor man's trail," since most stampeders lacked horses, money to hire them, and the toll fee for the Skagway Trail.

Because the Klondike River was in Canada, gold hunters had to cross the border, where Canadian Mounties required everyone to have a year's worth of food—about 2,000 pounds. A Klondiker's gear and food was called his "outfit," and it took about twenty trips to pack all of this from the start of the trail to the Canadian line. Packers-for-hire were available in Dyea, but the majority of those on the Chilkoot moved their own outfits. Most men carried eighty-five-pound loads, and women typically packed about thirty-five pounds. A Klondiker needed a traveling partner to guard his gear and food while he went back to the beginning of the trail for another load. In some cases traveling partners were spouses and children; others met loners along the way and partnered up with them. Great piles of supplies lay on the Dyea beach, including wooden boxes, flour sacks, tools, and stoves. A few piles displayed signs reading "Outfit for Sale Cheep."

The Chilkoot Trail wound steadily upward through the woods. Hikers watched their feet, following the beaten trail in the snow while taking care not to bump into the person in front of them. If they were lucky, they made it to Canyon City in a day. There, they pitched a tent and fell into a deep slumber. From Canyon City, it was a 5-mile trek to the next tent city, Sheep Camp, and then another three steep miles to the Scales, where an actual scale hung from a great, tipi-like frame. Here, people who had hired packers in Dyea had to weigh their supplies again, because the packers charged additional money to carry loads beyond this point. Scattered about on the ground were items that now seemed frivolous—fine china, rocking chairs, and doorknobs. From the Scales, hikers could look up at the Golden Stairs of the Chilkoot Pass.

The view was not for the faint of heart. The Stairs were a series of steps cut into the ice of the mountainside, and it stretched upward for 1,000 feet. Every twenty steps there was an ice bench where travelers could stop to rest and to catch their breath. A man stood at the bottom of the stairs collecting tolls, for it was he who had cut the steps into the ice, and he would re-cut them after every snowstorm.

Cheapskates were free to cut their own steps elsewhere on the pass, but the process was so slow that they inevitably returned to the Golden Staircase.

At the top of the stairs, the Klondiker dropped his load, slid down, picked up more of his belongings, and did it again. If a climber was strong, he could make two or three trips a day. He would need to make at least twenty trips to haul all his things up to the top. Once there, Canadian Mounties checked his outfit and, if he had the required 2,000 pounds of food, allowed him to enter the Yukon. From that point it was sixteen more chilly miles of Chilkoot Trail to the first Canadian lake, and once on the lake, the life of a Klondiker suddenly became a bit easier. He stopped hiking and hauling, and started building a boat that would hopefully carry him the remaining 560 miles to the Klondike.

The summer of 1897 was powered by gold fever and the Chilkoot Trail was crowded. The traffic on the trail slowed down as summer turned to fall and early winter, but it picked up again in March 1898. Thousands of hikers hoped to be at the Canadian lake and have a boat built before the lake ice broke in May. Though at first it might have seemed insane to attempt the Chilkoot when snow still covered the rocks, in fact it was an extremely good choice. The trail was incredibly rocky in summer, but the winter snow made it much smoother. One could pull a sled over the lower trail in winter, and fortunately this snow didn't melt until May.

Several enterprising folks had begun to make a living off of these travelers, and restaurants and hotels sprang up along the trail. Although the food was rarely good and the accommodations were poor, the merchants charged and received exorbitant sums. Frugal hikers walked past the restaurants to set up their camp stoves and cook beans, boil dried apples, and fry dough. This diet, however, was hardly enough to fuel the body for exertion. Tired hikers stumbled on snow-covered boulders, twisting ankles and breaking legs. Old people pushed their hearts until they burst. A thief shot himself rather than be caught by an angry mob. Hiking partners argued until they broke up, splitting their outfits to the point of cutting their tent in half. At least one marriage ended on the trail. While small dramas happened every day, seasons passed without a major disaster. That was about to change.

Heavy, wet snow fell on April 2, 1898, covering the piles of food sacks and the tent city at the bottom of the pass. Native packers called it "hi-yu snow," or high snow, and the next morning they refused to pack up the steep Chilkoot Pass. They knew that the fresh snow would destabilize the old snow and it could all come sliding down. Signs cautioning people not to hike were posted, but the morning after the snowfall, several restless men decided to ignore the warnings and take advantage of the traffic-free conditions on the stairs.

After the sun rose, they put on their backpacks and made a dash up the Golden Staircase. As they climbed, their boots slapped the ice and their voices lifted and carried along the wall. No one will ever know if it was the noise they made or the weight of their steps on the great wall of ice that somehow dislodged a mass of heavy snow at the top of the pass. First the cornice, then the entire wall of snow tumbled down the slope, sweeping the climbers off the wall and burying them, as well as all the people sleeping in their tents below. The slide raged like thunder, punctuated by the screams of people. As the powder settled and the snow quieted, there were still the moans and wails of victims. Those who had managed to avoid being buried came running with shovels and started digging.

Word spread along the trail, and a doctor was among the several hundred who raced to the rescue from Sheep Camp. All who came brought shovels and picks. The first person the doctor dug out was a woman, buried head down in the snow. Once free, she shook and cried without stopping. Similarly, many of those dug out alive were unhurt, but shaking with fear and cold. They had seen death and lived! Survivors were found all day. They told rescuers that the porous old snow had allowed easy breathing, but was so stiff they could not move a finger. Most of those rescued said they had slept in the snow. Others had talked the entire time: shouting for help, praying to God, or talking with other snowbound victims.

A full two days after the avalanche, an ox was found in a snow cave, calmly chewing its cud. No human survivors were found after the first day. Although digging continued, the rescue mission had become a recovery mission. The dead, some frozen in the act of running, were piled on sleds. One string of sleds held seventeen bodies. A Sheep Camp cabin became a storage place for the bodies, while friends and strangers tried to decide what to do with them. Some of the bodies were never identified, and even the number of victims was unclear, ranging from forty-nine to over seventy. Some bodies were sledded back to Dyea. Traveling partners took their dead friends and family members home for burial. So many bodies were buried in the Dyea cemetery that it became known as the Slide Cemetery. A few unidentified bodies were buried in a shallow grave near the Scales, until the summer snow melt uncovered them. That summer's Chilkoot hikers were met by yet another grisly sight: as the ice along the trail melted, arms and faces reached out of the snow. In all, seven new bodies were found that summer.

The Great Slide scared many people away from the Chilkoot Trail. Some, having seen the horror of April 3, returned home. Most newcomers chose to hike the Skagway Trail, thinking it was safer. Dyea and the Chilkoot Trail faded from use.

Today, the U.S. National Park Service and Parks Canada watch over the trail. Modern Chilkoot hikers need a permit and typically take three days to hike the 33 miles. Along the way the hikers see busted sleds, horse skeletons, worn-out boots, and broken china.

SOAPY SMITH SHOT IN SKAGWAY

- 1898 -

Skagway

SOAPY SMITH, PERCHED HIGH UP ON A WHITE STALLION, led the 1898 Fourth of July parade down Skagway's Broadway. He was the parade's grand marshal, but many in the crowd wondered what trick had landed him the honor. Only three days earlier someone else had been slated for that role. True to his name, Soapy was slick, and this wasn't the first time he had proven it! Most of Skagway wanted nothing more than to be rid of him.

Soapy's given name was Jefferson Randolph Smith Jr. He had learned to talk people out of their money in Colorado, where one of his scams was to sell soap for the high price of $5.00. As people watched, he appeared to be tucking $100, $50, and $20 bills under the wrappers of some bars. The naive audience failed to see him slide most of the bills up his sleeve, and they were also unaware that the first customer, who discovered a $50 bill tucked inside his soap, was really a member of Smith's gang. Customers rushed to buy the soap, but their own bars had no bonus money. The scam earned Smith the nickname of "Soapy."

Even though Soapy put a lot of time into his cons, his earnings were small, and he was eager to make some real money. A determined man, if not an honest one, he intended to be the first thief in an Alaska gold rush town. In 1896, Soapy relocated to Skagway, a port town where people began their long trek to the Klondike gold field. Soapy was sure he could own this new town—and he was right!

The Klondike gold rush of 1897–1898 was a mad stampede. One hundred thousand people tried to get to the gold field. They hadn't expected the trip to be so hard, though, and less than half of them made it to the Canadian Klondike. One of the reasons the trail was so difficult was that each stampeder had to have 2,000 pounds of supplies before entering Canada, and the Canadian Mounties stood guard at the border, making sure each person had the required burden. The trail north from Skagway was called the White Pass Trail, and it took a man with a packhorse ten trips to move all of his belongings up the 41-mile trail to the first lake. That was nine trips back to Skagway, and nine opportunities for Soapy's gang to lighten the man's pockets of his cash.

Newcomers were called "Cheechakos," a derivation of the word "Chicago." They were thought to be too trusting for their own good, and they were easy marks for Soapy's gang. Jeff Smith, as Soapy was known in Alaska, appeared to be the perfect gentleman. He had a Southern drawl and good manners, and his black beard was neatly trimmed. He wore a dark suit, white shirt, and tie, which he topped off with an odd, wide-brimmed hat that made him look harmless. He was nearing fifty, old enough to be a father figure for many new-comers. Most of his men wore proper suits and bowler hats, but sported names like Sheeney Kid and Fisco Red. The Smith gang had a small building with a sign reading Telegraph Office. There was always a line of Cheechakos in front, writing short notes home. The customer paid the clerk for each letter he'd printed and the clerk then clicked the message letter-by-letter on the telegraph lever. The young man left happy, never realizing the telegraph office was a fake and his message would never reach its intended receiver.

Soapy was quickly gaining confidence in his scams and decided to up the ante a bit. He had a hunch that if you were patriotic, other Americans would think you were honest. At his saloon, Jeff Smith's Parlor, he displayed a flag near the bar, and in the parlor's backroom there was even a live bald eagle. Intrigued by the bird, many a man foolishly went to the backroom to see it. There they were greeted not only by the bird, but also by a handful of men who took whatever money the man had. This was out-and-out robbery, but so far the gang was getting away with it.

Although most people traveled through Skagway, a growing number of people were staying in town to open honest stores, hotels, and restaurants. Some of the buildings were quite attractive, with false fronts and large windows. Business owners were trying to shape the wild boomtown into a classy city, and Skagway was calling itself the "San Francisco of the North." The honest residents of Skagway were growing tired of Soapy's crooked ways. He was giving the town such a bad name that many Klondikers stayed away, and it was not easy to make a living in an empty town.

In March 1898, a group calling itself the "Committee of One Hundred and One" posted the following message on walls around Skagway:

WARNING: ALL CONFIDENCE, BUNKO, and SURE THING MEN and all other objectionable characters are notified to leave Skagway and White Pass Road IMMEDIATELY and REMAIN AWAY. Failure to comply with this warning will be followed by PROMPT ACTION.

Soapy answered by hanging posters of his own, saying he spoke for the "law and order society consisting of 317 citizens." He called the Committee of 101 "blackmailers and vigilantes," and warned of quick legal action if they harmed "law-abiding citizens." Soapy was on guard but not reformed.

On July 7, 1898, just a few days after Soapy rode like a peacock through the streets of the city as the grand marshal, one of his gang invited J.D. Stewart into Jeff Smith's Parlor. Stewart was a miner fresh from the gold field, and he carried the gold he had found in a leather bag called a "poke." He was more than willing to talk to Soapy's man, who had said he was a major gold buyer. Stewart walked into the saloon's backroom to see the eagle. There, two thugs jumped him and stole his poke. He claimed that it held fifteen pounds of gold, worth $2,670, an enormous sum at the time. Stewart went straight to the U.S. Marshal seeking justice, but the officer did nothing. Stewart figured that the marshal was in Soapy's pocket, and this made him really mad. He walked into every store, restaurant, and saloon in Skagway and told his story. A crowd of angry Skagway citizens marched down to Soapy's saloon and found him inside behind the bar. He promised the group that Stewart would have his poke back by four that afternoon. Soapy stayed in the parlor and drank one shot of whiskey after another. Four o'clock passed and the poke did not appear. When a newsman predicted he'd face big trouble, Soapy raised his glass and answered, "By God, trouble is what I'm looking for!" The reporter returned to his office to work through the night. His story blared from the front page of the Skagway News the next morning. Clearly, the newspaper was siding with those who wanted to break Soapy. Tension was growing by the hour.

At eight o'clock the next evening, a group of citizens met on one of Skagway's piers. They intended to solve the Soapy problem one way or another. Fearing Soapy's gang would show, town surveyor Frank Reid stood guard with a .38-caliber revolver. A very drunk Soapy Smith marched down Broadway to the wharf, waving a rifle. Reid blocked him, and the two men swore and shouted at each other. Soapy hit Reid with the barrel of his Winchester, and Reid grabbed the gun barrel, pushing it down. When Soapy pulled the trigger, a bullet tore through Reid's groin. Frank Reid fired two or three shots in return. One bullet went through Soapy's heart and he died immediately. Reid dropped down in excruciating pain. The townspeople picked up their bleeding hero and carried him to the doctor's office, where he lay in great pain for twelve days before dying.

Soapy's body remained on the dock for three days. Following the shooting, many members of Soapy's gang had scattered to the woods. Twenty-seven of them were quickly rounded up. Stewart's poke of gold was found in the backroom of Smith's Parlor. Stewart was thrilled to get it back, but claimed $600 worth of gold dust was still missing.

Smith and Reid are buried in the Skagway Cemetery. Only a simple, cheap wooden board marks Soapy's grave, while Reid's grave has a giant stone monument, fit for a hero. It declares, "He gave his life for the Honor of Skagway."

Skagway did clean up and become an honest town, and the local businessmen were satisfied with what they saw. Unfortunately for them, gold was found in Nome, and in 1899 thousands left the Klondike for Nome. The Klondike gold rush was over. Even so, Skagway refused to die. The town quickly turned to tourism.

In the 1920s, a local entrepreneur turned Jeff Smith's Parlor into a museum. When the museum was no longer generating money, a lock was put on the door and the building was passed to another Skagway resident. Skagway is once again a tourism haven, and many today see Jeff Smith's Parlor from the outside, but the current owner only opens it to special guests. When visitors do walk in and adjust their eyes to the dim light, they see a mechanical mannequin of Soapy in a black suit, leaning on the dusty bar with a whiskey glass in his hand. He seems lost in thought until his head turns and his red eyes light up. Soapy is still tricky—even in death!

HARRIMAN BAGS HIS BEAR

- 1899 -

Kodiak

IN 1899, AMERICA'S RICHEST RAILROAD MAN traveled to Alaska to shoot a bear. Edward Harriman never did anything in a small way, and it wouldn't have occurred to him to hunt for a bear anywhere but on Kodiak Island, where Alaska's largest brown bears lived.

Harriman's New York doctor had told him to take a vacation from work and to get some rest. In response, Harriman rented a large steamship, fixed it up for luxury travel, and decided to go bear hunting in Alaska. Mrs. Harriman liked adventure, and it was decided that she and their children would go along also. Knowing that the trip would be long, they invited friends so that Mrs. Harriman would have female company. For the bear hunt Harriman brought a guide, packers, and a taxidermist. He suspected there were unnamed animals, plants, and glaciers in Alaska so he decided to bring along a team of scientists as well.

Harriman's list of Alaska-bound scientists grew to include twenty-five of America's most famous, among them: the chief of the U.S. Biological Survey; the director of the California Academy of Sciences Natural History Museum; the editor of *Forest and Stream;* plus the founders of the Arctic Club, Sierra Club, Boone and Crockett Club, Audubon Society, and American Forestry Congress. Two artists and a photographer were included for good measure. The two-month trip was called the Harriman Alaska Expedition. From Seattle to the Bering Sea and back, they covered 9,000 miles and stopped fifty times. The bear hunt was Harriman's most important stop.

On the morning of July 1, the ship was in a bay on Kodiak Island. Harriman went ashore with the ship's hunting guide, packers, a Kodiak Island hunter, and others. The island was a rolling sea of thick grass. The crew pitched several big canvas tents, laid out a table and chairs, and set up a wood stove with a tall chimney. They even had a tablecloth! This was camping in style. Meanwhile, Harriman and his guides hiked high and low over the hills, looking for a bear. They found none and returned to camp for the night.

Trying again the next day, it wasn't long before they spotted a golden-brown hump moving in the tall grass. A female Kodiak brown bear was grazing with her cub. In early July, the male and largest female bears gather along early-run salmon streams. The larger bears don't give the smaller bears much opportunity to fish, so the smaller bears have to wait for the larger ones to have their fill before it is their turn. On this day, this small female and cub chose to eat grass rather than wait for the larger bears to finish fishing. She had not started to grow her winter coat, and looked almost scruffy. However, there were no hunting laws, and a hunter could shoot any animal he wanted, at any time. If Harriman saw a better bear later, he could kill it also. Everyone readied their rifles, in case the bear charged. They knew that female bears guarded their cubs fiercely.

Harriman bravely walked ahead. The bear kept grazing. She had not yet seen him. He steadied his gun, lined up the barrel, and pulled the trigger. The beast dropped dead, and the cub cried out. Harriman quickly sighted his gun on the cub and pulled the trigger again. The cub fell as well. It was all over. Harriman had killed his bear!

The men grouped together to study the trophy, and they took a photograph of the bear lying in the grass. Her face was dish-shaped, and her ears were round. Her hind paws looked almost like human feet. The nails and teeth were huge. She weighed about as much as three men. The cub had been born the winter before. He was the size of a large dog.

One of the members of the hunting party returned to camp, requesting assistance in carrying the trophy back to camp. Two men headed over the hills to help. All Harriman wanted was the bear's cape; he was not interested in the meat. With a sharp knife, a slit was made down the bear's belly and the skin was cut from the carcass, with the head and paws attached. The men estimated that the large cape weighed 200 or 300 slippery pounds. This was packed back to camp. The cub was carried back whole.

Harriman, with the bear cape, returned to the ship that afternoon. Proudly he displayed his trophies to those on board. Harriman's two young sons were eager to touch the bears, and a photograph was taken of the baby bear leaning against a guest. Most were aware that the mother bear was small for a Kodiak brownie. The taxidermist would prepare the trophy on board, as it would be several weeks before they were home. He would flesh and tan the skin to make it into a rug or stretch it over a wooden "bear" form. The scientists were glad that Harriman had gotten his bear, as they could now focus on other things.

The ship was virtually a "floating university." Everyday there was friendly talk between the amazing scientists on board. This was an age of eager scientific collecting for museums, and at each of the fifty stops, scientists rushed ashore to collect samples of birds, worms, mammals, plants, and fossils. Hundreds of samples were gathered. Conservation was a relatively new idea and was discussed for hours. For example, most on Harriman's steamship believed that Alaska did not have an endless supply of plants and animals. However, there was no clear consensus on what should be done about that. Several of the scientists were concerned that the expedition had not seen a single sea otter. They were aware that otters were common in the past, and the fact that they appeared to be gone worried many. In addition, the over-fishing near a fish cannery shocked some. Would Alaska salmon soon die out?

The ship sailed along the coast to the town of Kodiak. There, the Harriman party celebrated the Fourth of July. Guests raised their glasses to toast the holiday and Harriman's bear. They played music on the gramophone that they had recorded earlier on wax records. One guest sat down at the ship's piano and played a few patriotic tunes. He was a skilled pianist, and many people sang along. The evening ended with a fireworks show over the water.

The ship continued to the Bering Sea. They sailed up as far as the Bering Strait, where Alaska and Siberia are very close. Edward Harriman never saw another bear. Toward the trip's end, they did stop at a Native Alaskan village. As no one was there, the expedition took half a dozen totem poles for museums.

The scientists were glad to have been part of this amazing trip. They had named many glaciers and had brought back hundreds of samples. Nearly 600 new plants and animals, including the ice worm, had been found. A tree, three animals, two fossils, a glacier, and a fjord were named after Edward Harriman. The expedition returned with 5,000 photographs and dozens of wonderful, lifelike bird drawings. Eleven books were written on the expedition's scientific discoveries. Later, laws were written to control hunting and protect native property.

Edward Harriman had his Alaskan brown bear and was happy. More importantly, because he took twenty-five scientists on his hunting trip, the nation's understanding of the glorious land of Alaska and the natural world in general took a huge leap forward.

RAILROAD WARS

- 1907 -

Valdez

EDWARD HASEY'S PALMS WERE SWEATY as he adjusted and readjusted his grip on his rifle. He had a bad feeling in the pit of his stomach, and it had been there for the past few days. He began to doubt the wisdom of what he was doing. He was just a railroad worker, for crying out loud! What had made it seem like a good idea to get deputized and defend a very valuable, and very controversial, parcel of land all by himself? The four-foot-high rock wall that he had built near where his tent was pitched was not going to protect him if an angry group of railroad men tried to take over.

Keystone Canyon, where Hasey was holed up, is one of the mountain passages between Valdez and the Wrangell Mountains. It was a very desirable spot to control in 1907, because it lay between two important destinations: the town of Valdez, which was the larger of the two port towns in Prince William Sound, and a very rich copper mountain deep in the heart of the Wrangells.

The Alaska Syndicate, a group of New York moneymen that included the Guggenheim brothers, was interested in the copper mountain. Known as the "Syndicate" or the "Guggs," they had millions of dollars to invest in their ventures. Those who weren't overly fond of the group likened them to an "eight-armed octopus," because it seemed the Guggs wanted to grab everything of value that Alaska had—including copper, gold, coal, fish canneries, railroads, and trading posts. Showing their financial muscle, the Guggs bought the Kennecott Copper Mine in the Wrangell Mountains. That was the easy part. Next they had to deal with the steep Wrangells, which flowed with glaciers and rivers. How would they get the copper ore to the coast?

At first, the Guggs looked at the shortest possible route for a railroad to link Valdez with Kennecott. At a bargain price they leased a strip of government land between the two locations. Ground was cleared, outcrops were dynamited, the grade was flattened, and a tunnel was blasted through a mountain. A level rail bed was made from Valdez to Keystone Canyon, a distance of nearly 20 miles. This was all very popular in Valdez, where residents figured the railroad would keep bringing jobs and money to the town.

It wasn't too long, though, before the Guggs scrapped the idea of connecting Valdez and the Kennecott mine by train. Cordova, the other town with a port in Prince William Sound, was selected as a replacement. The people of Valdez saw their jobs and money moving across the sound. The new Cordova-Kennecott route was longer (nearly 200 miles total), but by following the Copper River, there were fewer mountains to cross. After the route was changed, the name of the Guggs' line became the Copper River and Northwestern Railway. The Guggs held the right-of-way leases for both the Cordova-Kennecott and Valdez-Kennecott routes. They had no plans to build a Valdez-Kennecott rail, but they didn't want any other company to build one either.

"Alaska for Alaskans" was the cry in Valdez, where locals were angry that the Guggs had moved their railroad project to Cordova, yet were still holding the Valdez-Kennecott right-of-way lease. It appeared that Washington, D.C., was not protecting the people of the Alaska Territory, whose governor had been handpicked by the president, rather than elected by Alaskans. There was no one speaking for Alaska in the United States Congress.

In Valdez, 500 men felt their jobs had been taken from them, and as they were stewing about what to do, a smooth-talking gentleman appeared on the scene. Henry Reynolds had ideas for a "homegrown" railroad. He was saying what Valdez wanted to hear, and began selling thousands of shares for a new railway called the Alaska Home Railroad. Some Valdez folks spent every dollar they had on Reynolds's railroad stock. Reynolds did not have government right-of-way leases for the entire route to the copper country, but he started roadwork anyway. He hired local men to clear trees, dynamite rock, and level grade. Reynolds also bought the Valdez newspaper, bank, hotel, and even a few streets. The Reynolds Alaska Development Company was soon running out of money, but still had lots of local support. Reynolds declared that his railroad would lay grade through Keystone Canyon without a government land lease. Look out!

Everyone knew that attempting to lay grade through Keystone Canyon would be a direct challenge to the Guggs and their Copper River and Northwestern Railway, since they held the government lease on the land. Most even thought that it could end in violence. Over the summer of 1907, as Reynolds's plan for his railway became more obvious, tensions grew between the railroad companies. In an area crowded with mountains and glaciers, Keystone was the only passage wide enough for a railroad, and Reynolds was determined to use it. Eventually, a U.S. marshal deputized Edward Hasey and authorized him to defend the land and himself with a rifle if needed.

It was between the canyon wall and the river, a space less than 40 feet wide, that Hasey set up his post.

On September 25, 1907, what everyone feared finally happened. A gang of angry Alaska Home Railroad men, maybe 200 strong, marched from Valdez to Keystone Canyon. They would take the canyon by force! Forget the right-of-way lease—it was a Washington, D.C., piece of paper anyway! As the trespassers marched toward the tent, they waved clubs, shovels, and picks. Deputy Marshal Edward Hasey was hidden behind the rock wall. He was greatly outnumbered and feared for his life. He couldn't see any guns, but that didn't mean there weren't any. When the line of men drew within 12 feet of his shelter, Hasey raised his rifle and fired. He hit one man, then a second and a third. The railroad men had expected a confrontation, but not this. They gathered up their wounded men and bitterly returned to Valdez.

A few days later, one of the three injured men died. This was proof to many Alaskans that the Guggs would stop at nothing, not even murder. The town of Valdez was near the boiling point. Reynolds owned the Valdez newspaper, so the report of the event was very one-sided. A Valdez photographer took pictures of the crime scene, with men standing in for Hasey and the victims. Arrows and notes were added: "Where marshal stood," "Where first man was shot," and "Cut in which the Home RY men were."

Could Hasey receive a fair trial in Valdez? Many thought not. The murder trial was moved to Juneau. Each side had several lawyers, and the trial dragged on for many weeks. It appeared that the Guggs had bribed a witness to say that the Alaska Home Railroad men had a rifle. However, the witness took the Guggs' money and snuck out of town without appearing in court. After the first jury found Hasey not guilty of murder, he was tried again. In the second trial, he was found guilty of assault. Hasey spent eighteen months in jail. Many Alaskans thought this was much too light a sentence.

The Alaska Home Railroad failed in late 1907. It had run out of money. The people of Valdez were very disappointed, and many were secretly pleased when Henry Reynolds was fired from the Reynolds Alaska Development Company. The next year, the government arrested him for mail fraud.

The Guggs moved their Alaska Syndicate main office to Cordova in 1908. The Copper River and Northwestern Railway was completed from Cordova to Kennecott in 1911. It cost $20 million and took 5,000 men to build. Copper ore from the Guggs' mine traveled by train to a waiting Guggs' ship in Cordova. Over time, little Cordova grew into a busy port town. The Kennecott Copper Mine operated into the 1930s and made $175 million for the Alaska Syndicate. After the mine was closed, the Guggs abandoned the Copper River and Northwestern Railway.

The shootout in Keystone Canyon stirred things up in Washington, D.C. In 1907, the Chugach National Forest was created to include 23,000 acres surrounding Prince William Sound. National Forest rules made it harder for mining and railroad companies to do as they pleased in the sound. In 1908, an Alaskan was appointed to the U.S. Congress. He could not vote, but he spoke for Alaska. Alaskans finally had a home-rule Alaska Territory government. Most importantly, starting in 1912, they could elect a legislature, which met in Juneau. Ironically, the lawlessness that led to the Keystone Canyon shootout eventually led to the rule of law in the Territory of Alaska.

MOUNT KATMAI ERUPTS

- 1912 -

Mount Katmai

Boom! Boom! Boom! From the Alaska Peninsula to the Alaska Panhandle, people were sure they were hearing gunshots. On the afternoon of June 6, 1912, Alaskans looked around to see where the noise was coming from. About every twenty seconds there was another boom. Hot, gray ash started falling from the sky. There were flakes smaller than rice and chunks larger than kettles. It stung the skin like the jabs of a needle. The air tasted of foul gases and made some people vomit. Across western Alaska, people covered their eyes and hid in their homes. The ground beneath their feet shook, paused, and shook again. Was the end of the world near?

A cluster of volcanoes juts from the landscape on the Alaska Peninsula, Mount Katmai and Novarupta Volcano among them. It was Novarupta that erupted on June 6, 1912. From a distance, it appeared that the smoke and lava was spewing from Mount Katmai, the taller peak, and the event came to be known as the "Mount Katmai Eruption." Most people had no experience with volcanoes and were slow to figure out what was happening. The noise and ash continued for three days while people, within 200 miles of Katmai, lived in total fear.

At 3:30 in the afternoon, ash first arrived at the Alutiiq village of Ukak, which is less than 60 miles inland from the volcano. The hot soot dusted the barabaras, the Alutiiqs' sunken houses with dome-shaped roofs. Fortunately most of the villagers from Ukak and the other south Alaska Peninsula villages were at Kaflia fishing. A few men were in the village, and they were packing up their belongings to join the others at fish camp. They looked up in time to see the mountain blow up. It spewed over with molten lava that poured down the mountainside, burning everything in its path. The entire mountain appeared to be on fire! The Alutiiqs had heard the elders talk about great eruptions, but had never witnessed one. The men jumped into their bidarkas and paddled downriver as quickly as possible to Bristol Bay.

Kaflia, on the coast, about 30 miles from the volcano, was a fish camp. For 400 years, Alutiiq people gathered at the camp every June to catch salmon and dry it for the winter. An increase in earthquakes that spring had drawn a greater number of people to the camp, since they hoped they would feel security in numbers when the next earthquake came. However, it wasn't an earthquake that shook them to their core in June of 1912. That year, there were about one hundred men, women, and children collected at Kaflia.

On June 6, the gray-black cloud spread over the fishing camp, and the children ran to the top of a hill to view the smoking mountain. They watched, in fascination, the amazing light show surrounding the peak. Parents madly collected dried fish from the racks and filled buckets with fresh water. They then called their children back to the barabaras. Even in their underground homes, their eyes stung and ash traveled up their noses. Soon they were wetting their clothes and holding them over their faces. A few people soaked moss and pressed it to their faces. The barabaras had no windows, and the people burned their whale-oil lanterns for light. Unable to see where it was going, a little bird flew into one barabara. The children washed the bird's eyes and kept him as a pet. Would they see sunlight again? They looked to the elders for answers.

After three days of hiding, the Kaflia families stepped out of their homes. The sky was no longer black or hailing ash, but they could hardly recognize their village, which was buried under three feet of grit. To the children it looked like snow. The thick ash floated on the water, along with the bodies of salmon, whales, and sea lions. The Alutiiqs suspected that their inland home villages were at least as devastated as Kaflia. Nine brave men left Kaflia Bay in three bidarkas to seek help in Kodiak Island. On June 12, rescue came on a tugboat, captained by a United States government man from Kodiak. The Kaflia people climbed aboard with their bedding, bidarkas, cooking pots, and dishes. They traveled to Afognak, Kodiak's sister island, where they would be safer.

Three days earlier, when the volcano erupted, the ash cloud had reached Kodiak Island at about 5:00 P.M. The town of Kodiak was 100 miles from the volcano. This was a community of two-story houses with glass windows and wood shingle roofs. People hid in their homes, but the ash and gases blew beneath the windows. Breathing became difficult. No one was sure where the volcano was, and some thought it was on Kodiak Island itself. A plan was made to take the people away from Kodiak.

Very early the next morning, there was a knock on the door of the schoolteachers' home near the beach. The town doctor led the two women teachers to a government ship, their escape boat. The women soaked cloths in cold water and wrapped several layers around their faces. Because of the blackness, they held hands and groped their way along fences toward the harbor. The ash was so thick that they reached the ship before seeing its searchlight. The ship blasted its horn, trying to alert others to the fact that a rescue was underway and if anyone wanted to leave the island, they needed to try to find the ship.

When there were 500 people on the ship, plus a large number of others on a barge, they left Kodiak. They weren't sure where to go, and they weren't sure they could navigate even if they had a predetermined destination. The passengers and crew could barely see through their tears and ash. Some curled up inside their blankets to keep the ash off, while others tried to do something useful, like shovel ash off the deck. They traveled only 2 miles before anchoring off of Woody Island. One sick, old woman had already died; it had been too hard for her to breathe. Everyone was in too much pain to travel farther. The sea was rough. They huddled at Woody Island for another day. Then the ash storm stopped.

On June 9, the ship and barge returned to Kodiak. A blanket of gray ash 18 inches deep covered everything. Some roofs were crushed by the great weight. Those who still had homes set to shoveling the ash out. This proved to be futile work, since wind kept blowing it back indoors.

Over 200 miles from Katmai, the gold miners on the northern Kenai Peninsula heard the booming on June 6. At first they thought it was a gunfight. Then they saw the trees wave back and forth, and the ground shook beneath their feet. Three days later the wind shifted. The sun became an odd gray-yellow and ash dropped from the sky. Two or three inches covered the ground, rusting their mining tools and machinery. It was another nine days before anyone came to the Turnagain Arm gold field and told the miners they were seeing the effects of the Katmai eruption.

Even in Juneau, which was 750 miles away from the volcano, people heard the noise of the eruption on June 6. It was a long time before they learned that Alaska had experienced a huge volcanic eruption. For the rest of the summer, small earthquakes shook coastal communities.

For most of Alaska, life went on as usual, at least after the ash was cleaned up. Unfortunately, Kaflia, Uyak, and three other villages on the Alaska Peninsula had to be abandoned. The villagers were given a new home 200 miles from Katmai, called Perryville. The government built frame houses for them, yet the Perryville Alutiiqs missed their snug barabaras. For several years, area salmon fishing was poor, and the people struggled to adjust.

The National Geographic Society wanted to study the volcano. This was one of the five largest recorded volcanic eruptions in history. In fact, no other volcano in the 1900s would surpass it in size. The society sent an expedition to Katmai each summer from 1915 to 1919. The crew included a photographer, and Americans were thrilled to see pictures of Katmai in *National Geographic*. It was an eerie landscape without trees or grass. Smoke rose from thousands of vents in the ground. The area behind the volcano was called the "Valley of 10,000 Smokes." It was compared to the Yellowstone landscape, and there was a cry to protect this special place. In 1918, President Woodrow Wilson recognized the area as the Katmai National Monument. The name was later changed to the Katmai National Park and Preserve.

The 1912 Mount Katmai Eruption was the largest recorded volcanic eruption in Alaska history. Even today, the landscape is strangely beautiful where lava once coated the ground. Areas dusted by ash have since become rich grasslands. About every decade another volcano erupts in Alaska. Alaskans compare each eruption to the Katmai Eruption and say, "No, this one isn't like the Big One."

TO THE TOP OF DENALI

- 1913 -

Mount McKinley

WHO SAYS YOU NEED GORE-TEX AND EXPERIENCE to climb the tallest peak in North America? A group of four men did it in 1913 with nothing but sheer grit and determination.

Denali is the "High One," the tallest mountain in North America. It towers over the Alaska Range, and on a clear day can be seen from hundreds of miles away. It was named "Mount McKinley" in 1896, to honor presidential candidate William McKinley. Although McKinley did win the presidency, many Alaskans still prefer the Athabaskan name for the mountain, Denali. Mountain climbers have always been drawn to it. Several well-equipped expeditions tried, but failed, to reach her highest peak in the early 1900s. In 1913, four Alaskans with little money and climbing experience took on the mountain. The members of the 1913 expedition were sure they knew the best route up Denali. They would carry more food than the other groups and were prepared to wait out a blizzard.

The 1913 climbing team did not inspire confidence at first glance. The only member of the team who had climbed before was Dr. Hudson Stuck, the fifty-year-old archdeacon, or head priest, of the Episcopal Yukon Mission. It was Stuck who scraped together $1,000 for food and supplies for an expedition that would take several months. It was also Stuck who selected the other members, chosen primarily because they were willing to go unpaid. Harry Karstens, age thirty-five, was stronger than Stuck and knew the area well. He delivered mail by dogsled between Fairbanks and the mining camps near Denali. He was the one who poled a boat upriver to stash the group's supplies near Denali before winter. Walter Harper, a twenty-one-year-old Athabaskan, was Stuck's dog handler, and Robert Tatum, twenty-one, was an Episcopal missionary in Nenana, a small community between Fairbanks and Denali. Two Athabaskan boys from the Nenana Mission, Esaias and Johnny, were invited also. They were only fourteen and fifteen. The two were thrilled, even though they were brought along to help, not to climb. All the other mission boys wanted to go on this adventure and were extremely jealous.

The group left Fairbanks by dogsled in March. They traveled over 150 miles on frozen rivers and through spruce forests. Two months later, they reached Denali and set up base camp. Stuck unpacked his camera and photographed his friends standing in front of their six-by-seven-foot canvas tent. Huge snowshoes were planted in the snow nearby. It must have been warm, as only Karstens wore a fur parka and cap. The others wore just wool pants and shirts and none of them had gloves on.

After the base camp was organized, Esaias said good-bye and left with the dogsled. He mushed all the way back to the Nenana Mission by himself, a distance of over 100 miles. Johnny stayed in base camp to watch after things. He would be on his own for over a month.

On April 11, Stuck, Karstens, Tatum, and Harper said farewell to Johnny and base camp. The weather was clear and the summer sun never set. They started snowshoeing up the mountain, walking up a glacier as if it were a wide highway. To their left was a ridge that dropped off steeply. The men were carrying a great amount of food, fuel, and heavy equipment. It took several days to ferry all of their supplies from one camp to the next. They set up a number of camps, each a couple hundred feet higher than the last.

On June 6, they were camping at the 18,000-foot level. At that high altitude, the air was thin and breathing was difficult. The temperature was twenty-one degrees below zero. They had two weeks' worth of food and fuel, enough to wait out a blizzard. Walter Harper was that night's cook. They were carrying a ten-pound bag of flour and wanted to use it rather than carry it farther. Their sourdough starter had failed, so Harper tried cooking noodles from scratch. He did not boil them long enough over the little coal-oil stove and the noodles were still doughy when they were served. After dinner, everyone crawled into the one tent to sleep. The same little stove that cooked their dinner heated the tent and their single bed was toasty and warm. The bed was actually fairly comfortable since it was made atop a pile of thick sheep and caribou skins. Blankets, down quilts, and a wolf robe were piled on top for warmth. However, Stuck, Karstens, and Tatum tossed all night with sick stomachs. Only Harper slept well.

At three the next morning, June 7, they woke to bright sunshine but a strong wind. After eating a light breakfast, they prepared for their dash to the summit. Daypacks were loaded with lunch and scientific gear. They hoped to summit the mountain and get back that day. Karstens's stomach still grumbled from the noodles. Stuck and Tatum had headaches, either from dinner or the thin air. Only Harper felt well enough to lead. The group formed a long line behind Harper and roped together. They were all warmly dressed. Stuck wore long underwear, moose-hide pants and a shirt, a thick sweater, and a fur parka. He had two pairs of mittens, one made of lynx fur. Instead of boots, he wore tall moccasins with six pairs of heavy socks. Everyone was dressed just as warmly, yet their hands and feet were numb with cold. The men agreed that cold temperatures felt worse at high altitudes.

They strapped on snowshoes, picked up ice axes, and started the walk up the ridge of the glacier's high basin. It was a slow and painful hike. When the climb became steep, they switched from snowshoes to metal crampons. Each breath was difficult, and the men walked with their mouths open, gulping air. After every twenty steps, Stuck's vision went black and he had to sit down. Their feet and hands did not warm up until noon. Harper continued to lead, and he took the heaviest items from Stuck's daypack and added them to his own. With his ice axe, Harper cut steps in a rough section of the ridge 3 miles long. The ridge ended in a horseshoe. Reaching the top of the horseshoe, they saw Denali's twin peaks, which are a mile apart. Here, the climbers finally found some shelter from the biting wind and stopped for lunch. They shared hot tea from a thermos bottle, which warmed them somewhat, but the men were still worried. Would they lose fingers or toes to frostbite? Should they turn back?

After coming so far, no one was in the mood to give up. The climbers pushed on to the taller of the two high points, the South Peak. They climbed step-by-step, as if on a staircase. It was Walter Harper who first stepped on the summit of Denali. Harry Karstens and Robert Tatum were soon beside him. The three pulled Hudson Stuck to the top. Success! Everyone shook hands in relief and joy, then joined in prayer, thanking God for their safe climb.

By this time it was 1:30 in the afternoon. The men quickly set up a little tent and performed some scientific tests. Tatum measured angles with a compass so that they could make a good map, while Stuck took photographs.

Only after they finished the tests did the climbers stop to enjoy the awesome view. The men felt so far above the earth, it was like being in heaven. At this high altitude, the sky was the deepest blue they had ever seen. They could see 100 miles or more in every direction. Only a forest fire haze kept them from seeing farther. Harper planted a tent pole into the snow. It became the flagpole for the little American flag Tatum had made from handkerchiefs. Stuck led them in a small climbers' prayer, and then the four hiked down the mountain. At 5:00, they stumbled into camp. Hudson Stuck wrote in his book, *The Ascent of Denali,* that this was the happiest day of his life.

Denali and the area around her became Mount McKinley National Park in 1917. Harry Karstens was the first man to manage the park and did so from 1921 to 1928. The park was enlarged and because many Alaskans still preferred the name Denali, the name was changed to Denali National Park and Preserve. Archdeacon's Tower, Karstens Ridge, Harper Glacier, and Mount Tatum were named to commemorate the 1913 pioneer climbers.

Interest in climbing Denali has increased greatly. Today, approximately 1,200 climbers attempt to reach the summit of North America's highest peak every year. Those who succeed do so in about eighteen days, yet they remain respectful of the 1913 pioneers.

SAVING NOME

- 1925 -

Nome

OPEN WIDE! NOME'S DOCTOR LOOKED INTO THE mouth of the six-year-old boy. What he saw was frightening—white sores in the back of the boy's throat, indicative of diphtheria. Just a few days earlier, Dr. Welch had visited two Inupiat children whose throats were so sore they could not open their mouths. They later died, and he now understood why. Diphtheria germs spread quickly and death could come in days. All the children of Nome, and many of the adults, would die unless treated with a vaccine. Dr. Welch quickly looked through his cabinets and drawers, and determined that he had enough to vaccinate this child and maybe four more. It was January 21, 1925, and the Bering Sea would be frozen for several months. There was very little hope of obtaining more serum in time to prevent a massive outbreak.

Nome, on the Bering Sea, had settled down since the excitement of the gold rush. The city's growth had stabilized at about 1,400 people. Dr. Curtis Welch was the only doctor. He had watched helplessly in 1918 as a flu epidemic swept through Alaska, killing entire villages. A diphtheria epidemic could do the same thing. Determined to do his best to prevent this, Dr. Welch sent an urgent telegraph to three Alaskan cities, asking for help.

Most of Alaska took notice. In Anchorage, the Alaska Railroad Hospital had plenty of diphtheria serum that they would be happy to give to Nome. A Seattle hospital promised to send more. Now the problem became how to get the vaccine to Nome. The Alaska Territory governor chose to give the task to the men who delivered the mail by dog team and asked the Northern Commercial Company to set up a dogsled relay in western Alaska. The U.S. Army Signal Corps offered to send messages between their few telegraph stations. Everyone wanted the "Mercy Race to Nome" to succeed!

An Anchorage doctor placed the serum in a cylinder, which was wrapped in a quilt and set in a canvas sack. This twenty-pound package was handed to the Alaska Railroad train conductor in Anchorage on January 26. From Anchorage, it traveled 220 miles by rail to Nenana, in the heart of Alaska's cold interior. However, Nome was still an incredible 700 miles away.

Twenty-one mushers with fast teams were positioned about 30 miles apart, each ready to run part of the trail. "Wild" Bill was the first dog musher. On January 27, he and his team of nine huskies were waiting by the Nenana track. It was a bit before midnight when the trail conductor handed him the package. The team took off in forty-below-zero blackness, but thankfully there was no wind. By traveling on the frozen Tanana River, they avoided the deepest snowdrifts. Wild Bill's leg of the journey was 52 miles, which he completed in about ten hours, before handing the package off to the next musher, Dan Green.

Green had a shorter run, but fought a strong wind much of the way. The wind caused his huskies to tangle their harness, and eventually he had to stop and take off his mittens to untangle them. Within moments, he felt his fingers tingle and looked down to see them turn from red to white. Frostbite! After meeting Johnny Folger's team at Manley Hot Springs, Green likely soaked in the hot water that bubbled from the earth in an effort to save his fingers.

Folger was a local Athabaskan, as were all the interior mushers that followed him. They didn't mind the extreme cold and Mother Nature seemed to be saving her stormiest weather for the coast. Upon completing his leg, Folger passed the package off to the fourth musher, Sam Joseph. The fifth team, Titus Nickolai's, reached the wide Yukon River, and from there, the serum exchanged hands no less than ten times before leaving the river with a musher who went by the name of "Jackscrew." Although it meant plowing back through the deep and windblown snow, Jackscrew pulled off the river and followed a direct route to the sea. As his dogs had a 40-mile leg, Jackscrew ran alongside his sled during half of it to lighten their load.

Victor Anagick, an Inupiat man was the fifteenth musher. With eleven huskies, he took the package to the coast. He handed it off to an Inupiat named Myles Gonangnan. This next leg of the trek was a hard 40-mile slog along the shore. The wind blew hard and since there were no trees to block it, the snow piled up in deep drifts. Gonangnan's dogs struggled through drifts four feet deep. At the village of Shaktoolik on January 31, the package was handed to Henry Ivanoff. He continued along the coast, fighting the wind, but about a half mile outside Shaktoolik, his team charged after a reindeer. Ivanoff had to stop his sled and try to untangle his dogs, who were fighting chaotically. Ivanoff was distressed to see that his leg of the journey had to come to a temporary halt while he calmed the dogs and set up his sled again. He knew that precious hours were ticking by.

Ivanoff wasn't the only one who was worried the package wouldn't make it all the way. Back in Nome, the people were worried as well.

Many had wanted to escape to mining camps or villages to shelter themselves and their children from the disease, but Nome was under quarantine and no one could leave. On January 30, three children and their mother came down with diphtheria. Dr. Welch had only three doses of medicine left and was in a bit of a predicament: how should he decide whom to treat? The woman took the problem out of his hands when she insisted that her children receive it. She would wait at the hospital for the rescue package. The people of Nome had no idea where the package was or how soon it would arrive.

Three Nome residents had eagerly volunteered to be part of the relay, and they waited anxiously for their turns to help. Their names were Leonhard Seppala, Gunnar Kaasen, and Ed Rohn, and when they knew the relay was underway, the three left Nome with their dogs. Rohn would wait at Point Safety, which would mark the beginning point for the last leg. Kaasen would take up his second-to-last position at Olson's Roadhouse, and Charlie Olson would wait at Dexter's Roadhouse. Seppala, the strongest musher, would follow the trail all the way from Nome to wherever he found the package; then he would turn around and bring it back to Olson for the final three legs of the journey. Seppala would travel a grueling 170 miles before he found the precious package and started his leg.

The wind was blowing hard along Norton Sound. Seppala almost didn't see Ivanoff and his stalled dog team in the whiteout. Ivanoff was happy to hand off the package. In an effort to save time, Seppala created a shortcut and crossed 20 miles of Norton Sound ice. This was a risky maneuver in a blinding blizzard on unstable sea ice. However, he trusted his lead dog, Togo, to find the way. Back on land, he watched the sea ice crack up behind him. Seppala found a sod igloo and after feeding the dogs, he pulled the sled into the shelter. Exhausted from the long trek, Seppala slept for a few hours, hugging the package to keep it warm. Early in the morning of February 1, he set off again.

When he finally reached Dexter's Roadhouse, the dogs dropped to the ground. They had raced 91 miles—all in a storm!

Charlie Olson and his team were waiting at Dexter's Roadhouse. The temperature was still deathly cold and the storm was raging. Strong gusts of wind blew Olson's sled and team off the trail more than once. His seven huskies were so cold that he stopped to put a blanket on each one. They wearily arrived at Olson's Roadhouse at 7:30 that evening. They had survived 25 miserable miles. Now it was Gunnar Kaasen's turn.

Kaasen hitched up his twelve huskies behind lead dog Balto and rode into the wild storm. The wind blew the ice clear in spots, while piling it 5 feet deep elsewhere. He hoped to stop at a village for a break, but missed it in the whiteout. Crossing a flat about midnight, a gust of wind flipped the sled. He struggled to right the sled and untangle the dogs, and then realized with a sense of doom that the package was nowhere to be found. Desperate, Kaasen yanked off his gloves and felt around with his bare hands until he found it. After this, the wind blew against his back propelling him forward. With the wind at last working in his favor, Kaasen made the next 12 miles in just eighty minutes. He arrived at Safety at 2:00 on the morning of February 2. Naturally, Ed Rohn was asleep, having no idea when to expect Kaasen and his team. To wait for Rohn to rise and ready his dogs would lose valuable time, and Kaasen trusted his team to take him the last 21 miles home.

Balto pulled the sled into Nome at 5:30 in the morning on February 2. Kaasen and Balto and the rest of the team had traveled 53 miles. They went straight to Dr. Welch's door and handed over the package, which was frozen but undamaged. Welch thawed out the serum and with a glad heart gave vaccinations to the Nome patients. Five children had died, but no more would. There would be no major epidemic. On February 21, Dr. Welch ended the Nome quarantine. The Mercy Race had saved Nome.

WELCOME BACK, MUSK OX

- 1930 -

Fairbanks

L. J. PALMER HEAVED A SIGH OF RELIEF. The second stage of his journey was nearly over, and he could almost begin the work that he loved to do. It was November 4, 1930, and he was on board the Alaska Railroad train with thirty-four Greenland musk oxen in crates.

In September, Palmer had met a Norwegian steamship in New York Harbor and stood by while the animals spent a month in quarantine. Then for another month, he traveled with them by train to Seattle and by steamship to Alaska. Not a single animal had died or suffered injury—so far. But the true test was only beginning. The question had never been "Can a Greenland musk ox survive the trip to Alaska?" What the U.S. government wanted to know was "Can a Greenland musk ox thrive in Alaska?" Palmer thought he knew the answer. After all, Alaska had had native musk oxen until they were hunted to extinction around 1865. However, it was 1930 and money was scarce due to the Great Depression. If musk oxen could help curb the effects of the Depression by providing a source of food, the government was willing to give it a try.

Eventually, the musk oxen arrived in College, outside of Fairbanks, where they were let loose in a forty-acre pen. There were nineteen females and fifteen males. Most of the animals appeared to be yearlings. They had been in crates for sixty days, and they looked rather awkward as they stretched their short legs, remembering how to walk and run. Curious about their surroundings, the musk oxen sniffed the snow on the ground, their breath rising in great puffs in the below-zero weather. Before long they wandered over to the few black spruce trees that dotted one end of the pen.

People surrounded the pen: college teachers and students, as well as visitors from Fairbanks. These odd creatures were a big event! The musk oxen look more like buffalo than oxen. Their hooves were goat-like, and both males and females had horns that curved like hefty bicycle handles. The huge hump over their shoulders made them appear powerful. Long black hair, as coarse as a horse's tail, hung down over their bodies. The appearance of their hair earned them the Inupiat name of "Omingmak," meaning "bearded one." They weren't large animals, and few were over 300 pounds. Smaller animals had intentionally been captured in Greenland, since the idea of transporting full-size wild bulls seemed needlessly difficult.

The U.S. Department of Agriculture's Biological Survey Station intended to study these animals closely, and if all went well, they would later be released on Nunivak Island, which had been made a National Wildlife Refuge in 1929. Palmer, a biologist, was in charge of the operation. One of his main research goals was to find out if these Greenland musk oxen would eat and thrive on Alaskan grass and moss. The station's biologists would watch them for a few years to find out. They would fill notebooks with facts on diet, mating, calving, and herd behavior.

No musk ox calves were born that first spring in 1931. The crew was disappointed, but they determined several reasons why that was the case. First, the animals had been captured during early fall, which is their breeding season. Second, the trip had been warm and stressful. Third, they were fed hay, an unfamiliar food. In fact, the researchers had to wait three more years before any calves were born. Finally, in the spring of 1934, seven five-year-old cows gave birth. The seven cute, fluffy creatures weighed about twenty-five pounds each. Later, the biologists learned that under ideal conditions, a three-year-old cow could become a mother. The biologists still had a lot to learn.

That first summer, 1931, the musk oxen were allowed to range in a fenced 7,500-acre pasture, near the station's reindeer field. The ground was hilly, grassy, and scattered with spruce trees. The animals learned to behave as a herd. When they felt threatened as a group, they bunched together and lowered their heads. All summer, the two largest males eyed each other, and by late summer they were ready to battle. From a great distance they lowered their heads and charged blindly. The two armored heads came together with great force, and the pounding could be heard a mile away. Luckily, a full 7 inches of horn and bone protect the animal's brain, and after every collision each bull shook his head and walked away before lowering their heads and charging again. They did this over and over until blood oozed from cuts. Eventually, both animals fell to the ground, and the crew could not save them. Both bulls died of their injuries. Everyone at the station was sad, but the crew had learned a lesson. In the future, they would try to keep large males apart.

The researchers knew that, in Greenland, musk oxen protect themselves against wolves. They wondered, though, if they could protect themselves against Alaskan bears, a very different kind of predator. That first summer the biologists found that these young adults could not. Two black bears entered the pen and killed two musk oxen. Moving the herd to Nunivak Island took on a greater urgency, since the enormous island had no predators at all.

The death of the four animals this first summer gave the biologists the opportunity to sample the meat. Palmer ate a musk ox steak, and he judged it to be as tasty and fine-grained as the best American beef. In his opinion, the Native Alaskans would definitely approve of the meat. In fact, it could be packaged and sold in stores. The more he thought about it, the more excited he became. This was a possible new cash industry for Alaska. Alaska could pull itself out of the Depression!

Palmer had another idea. Could musk ox wool be used for something? The oxen's long hair served as a kind of raincoat for the animals, but under that was a layer of super-soft wool. The wool was only about 2 inches long, but it kept the animal warm in sub-zero weather. In the spring, each animal shed a few pounds of this fluffy fiber, and Palmer collected it and gave it to a national wool mill. The mill's lab chemist studied it and discovered that it was eight times warmer than sheep's wool. The chemist even declared it to be better than cashmere.

Palmer and others immediately began brainstorming ideas for what musk ox wool could be called. They knew that many arctic animals had a downy undercoat to keep them warm. The Inupiat word for down was "qiviut," and this was the name chosen for the soft gray-brown undercoat of the musk ox.

The Alaska Agricultural College and School of Mines had both a Home Economics Department and a U.S. Department of Agriculture Cooperative Extension Service. Several pounds of musk ox wool were given to Lydia Fohn-Hansen, an instructor at the college, who picked out the coarse guard hair by hand and spun it into yarn on a spinning wheel. The fine, gray-brown yarn looked very promising. Fohn-Hansen taught her students to knit socks, gloves, and mittens. They also learned to use looms, weaving the wool into scarves. In the end, the garments were very soft, but if tightly knit, the garments were even too warm for Fairbanks! A lacy knit was declared best. Amazingly, these lacy knit scarves weighed less than three ounces. Soon, people in Fairbanks wanted to buy them. Home Economic students started making and selling the scarves, and the money they earned was reinvested in more spinning wheels and looms. Paid work during the Great Depression—this was wonderful!

In 1931, the U.S. Department of Agriculture gave the Biological Survey Station to the Alaska Agricultural College and School of Mines. Alaskan college students studied gold mining, reindeer herding, musk ox care, and qiviut spinning. Despite the Depression, Alaskans felt hopeful.

In 1935, the biologists concluded that the animals might survive in Alaska's arctic region. Since it also appeared that the U.S. government would soon stop funding the project, the time seemed ripe for sending four musk oxen to Nunivak Island. Much to everyone's relief, they survived the winter. Feeling hopeful, the rest of the herd was shipped to Nunivak in 1936. A few died that year, which was disappointing, especially since everyone had grown attached to the great beasts. However, the good news was that most of the herd had survived.

Could Greenland musk oxen thrive in Alaska? L. J. Palmer had answered the question with a resounding yes. Descendants of that first herd still roam Nunivak Island today and are doing well as transplants on the mainland of western Alaska. There are well over 600 animals in the state. Inupiats hunt the beasts, collect the qiviut, and knit the fiber into lacy scarves.

JAPANESE CAPTURE KISKA ISLAND

- 1942 -

Kiska Island

LIEUTENANT WILLIAM HOUSE, OF THE U.S. NAVY, fastened a white rag to a stick and prepared to walk the many miles that separated the cave he had lived in for the past fifty days from the very people he had been evading. While he was not eager to be a war prisoner of the Japanese, he was less eager to die. He had cursed the midsummer sun, which stayed out all night and kept his foraging forays relatively close to the safety of his cold, damp cave. On bright nights he had rushed out around midnight, counting on the fact that the Japanese soldiers had to sleep sometime, and eaten whatever grass and worms he could find. On foggy nights he crawled out on the beach, where there were small creatures to be found in the sand and under rocks. He dug for clams, broke the shells, and ate them raw. Critons, resembling single-shelled oysters, clung stubbornly to boulders. He pried them off and sucked their meat.

Even with these extreme efforts, House knew he was near starvation. Daily he was tempted to look for the emergency supplies he and his men had stationed around the island, but his fear of being detected kept him from traveling too far. When he finally trudged into the Japanese camp on July 28, his friends who were being held prisoner there hardly recognized him. Weighing less than a hundred pounds, he looked like an old man, and his long beard could not hide his sunken cheeks. His arms and legs were extremely thin, and ragged clothes hung from his body. Much to his surprise, the Japanese fed him and nursed him back to health.

House's ordeal had started with a radio warning that was heard at the navy's weather station on Kiska Island. He and his crew of nine men, dubbed the Kiska Ten, were posted on this small, remote island and were the westernmost post of America's secret Aleutian Campaign to protect the Alaska Territory from Japan. Their camp, which was on the rolling tundra below Kiska Volcano, included two cabins and a radio shack connected by a boardwalk. Their task was to measure and record the temperature, wind speed, rain, and snow. Since the Aleutians are very windy and rainy, this was useful information for pilots. House and his crew had a secondary mission as well: they secretly reported on any Japanese ships and planes in the area. They kept codebooks full of words to use on the radio, to confuse any Japanese who might be listening.

House was twenty-nine and his men were also young. They enjoyed the adventure of Kiska Island life, exploring the 110-square-mile treeless island's mountains, canyons, and beaches. No one else lived there, but fishing and navy boats occasionally visited the island. The Kiska Ten had posed for a photograph earlier that summer. Navy men all, they did not dress the part. They wore non-military jackets and only half of them had hats. Several had started growing beards and letting their crew cuts grow out. House was the shortest man, solidly built but with no excess fat. Beardless and wearing a hood that covered his sandy hair, he looked more like a radioman than an officer. A black husky pup named Explosion kept the men company and had been given to them by an officer at an Alaskan navy base.

On June 3 and 4 of 1942, House and others who were posted up and down the Aleutian Chain heard the same news over the radio: the Japanese were bombing the army-navy base at Dutch Harbor, located on the eastern end of the chain. House was alarmed by the news on the radio. He knew that Japanese planes had bombed the U.S. naval base at Pearl Harbor on December 7, 1941, and he quickly readied his men for a Japanese attack on Kiska Island. June 5 and 6 were stormy days, which pleased House, since the weather was too rough for Japanese planes. He gave one man radio duty and had the other men slosh around in the rain, hiding emergency supplies at several sites on the island. They decided that the island's caves were perfect places to stash food, camp stoves, fuel, blankets, and first-aid kits. Everything was hidden by the evening of June 6. The men laid their sleeping bags side-by-side in the tiny radio shack, and the dog, Explosion, curled up with them. By midnight they were all asleep. Rain pounded on the roof.

At 2:15 on the morning of June 7, the men awoke to the horror of machine-gun bullets splintering the walls of their shack. One of the men, Winfrey, was struck in the leg and blood soaked his sleeping bag. A bullet tore through the hand of another man, Courtenay. House pulled open the door and ordered his men to escape. Explosion ran out, yelping. Eight men crawled from the shack into the thick fog. House and a man named Turner remained behind for a few minutes, burning the secret codebooks and smashing the radio so it wouldn't fall into the hands of the enemy. Then the two crawled out of the building.

On the tundra, Japanese soldiers soon surrounded poor Winfrey. Six Japanese ships sat in the cove, and 1,250 soldiers were positioned onshore. The Americans were outnumbered 125:1. Winfrey was hauled down to the beach. The Japanese set up a little tent in the rain and carried him inside. A Japanese doctor entered the tent and opened a surgeon's bag. He skillfully removed the bullet from Winfrey's leg. This was not the treatment Winfrey had expected!

The Japanese found a second American sailor that day. After several hours, they also found all of the hidden emergency supplies. Japanese troops stood guard at each of the supply stashes in wait for the Americans. Over the next few days, seven more Americans were found or surrendered. Only William House remained free. While they waited for House to emerge from whatever hiding spot he had found, the Japanese made themselves comfortable on the island.

On June 7, the day of the Kiska Island attack, the Japanese also attacked Attu Island. Twelve hundred Japanese troops captured Attu's forty-four Aleuts, the schoolteacher, and his wife. The teacher died, either at the hands of the Japanese or his own. The other Attu captives were shipped to Kiska Island. After House was captured, there were a total of fifty-five prisoners on Kiska. All were sent to Japan, where they worked in prisoner labor camps until the end of the war.

Attu and Kiska were the only Alaskan islands occupied by the Japanese during World War II. The Japanese gave Kiska a Japanese name, Miokodo Island, and brought in more troops until the island population numbered 2,500. They built bunkers and an airstrip, and before long the island sported many trucks, pieces of heavy equipment, fourteen airplanes, and at least three submarines. This was their base to take over the Aleutian Islands and then North America. From Kiska Island, they bombed coastal targets in Alaska, Canada, Oregon, and California. The Japanese knew America wasn't going to give up the Aleutians easily, and it wasn't long before the Japanese radio on Kiska detected American planes overhead. They braced themselves for counterattacks.

During the war, 144,000 American troops were sent to Alaska. America built more than 300 military bases in the territory, several of them in the Aleutian Chain. Nearly 27,000 servicemen were stationed on a new base on an island east of Kiska and Attu. On every fog-free day, American planes bombed Attu and Kiska islands. In the single month of April 1943, Kiska was bombed eighty-three times with 640 tons of material.

The only hand-to-hand fighting on North American soil during World War II took place in the Aleutian Islands. In May 1943, 10,000 U.S. troops attacked Japanese-controlled Attu Island. After several days of battle, America finally won back the island. The Battle of Attu cost 549 American and 2,350 Japanese lives. Only twenty-nine Japanese soldiers were alive after the battle was over. In August 1943, over 35,000 American and Canadian troops landed on Kiska Island. They expected a fight as bloody as the Battle of Attu. Instead, a friendly husky, Explosion, greeted them on the beach. There was not a single Japanese soldier on the island! Weeks earlier, they had secretly left Kiska Island. The entire Aleutian Chain belonged to the United States again!

The same navy officer who had given Explosion to the Kiska Ten rescued the dog. The Kiska Ten and most of the Attu villagers survived their imprisonment in Japan and returned home to America. Attu Island was so damaged that the twenty-four returned Attu villagers settled on a neighboring island. After the war, William House served the U.S. Navy until he retired in the 1960s. Kiska Island and seven other Alaskan war sites were honored as National Historical Landmarks in the 1980s.

Today, Kiska is still littered with bomb-damaged Japanese trucks, submarines, and ships. Many of the U.S. bases built in Alaska during World War II were used during the Cold War with the Soviet Union. Some of those bases are still operating today. Not many people visit Kiska today, but a stroll along the island's quiet shore, amid the refuse of war, easily calls to mind the lonely and desperate days of William House.

BARROW DUCK-IN

- 1961 -

Barrow

HARRY PINKHAM STOOD OUTSIDE HIS OFFICE BEWILDERED. In the street were 300 men, women, and children, and each of them was holding a dead duck. There were old grandmothers and little children who smiled sweetly while gripping the illegal birds. Harry wasn't sure what was going to happen next, but he knew it would involve lots of paperwork and lots of time. And he knew he was in this mess alone.

When Alaska became the forty-ninth state in 1959, the federal government began to take more than a passing interest in the area. In 1961, the secretary of the interior decided it was time to start enforcing the Protection of Migratory Bird Treaty in Alaska. The U.S. had signed the treaty with Canada and Mexico in 1916. It was intended to protect ducks and geese in the arctic from March 10 to September 1. The birds could be hunted during the rest of the year, but this would have had little impact on the bird population because most of the birds would have already flown south.

When federal game wardens enforced the summer bird-hunting ban, Native Alaskans were shocked and angry. They had always hunted for meat. Their subsistence hunting lifestyle was at the core of their culture, and the meat-rich diet kept them strong, healthy, and warm.

Their anger and distress over the new regulations became so acute that on the Yukon-Kuskokwim Delta, a few natives shot at game wardens. In the village of Barrow, the people weren't ready to be quite that extreme, but they were completely unwilling to bend their traditions and needs to fit the ideas of a government body thousands of miles away.

Barrow is a large Inupiat village on the Arctic Ocean, where the people depend on birds, caribou, polar bear, fish, and whale. Most of these animals migrate to the arctic only during the summer when the water is free of ice. For example, ducks arrive each May and are gone by mid-September. This means that for four months, the wetlands surrounding Barrow are alive with ducks and geese. In the spring of 1961, the villagers were eager for the first wave of ducks to arrive. Barrow's game warden, Harry Pinkham, was new to game law enforcement, but not to Alaska. He liked the Arctic and its people, but "going by the book" would be a challenge.

On May 20, Pinkham saw a Barrow man hunting geese on the tundra. As the law required, he took the man's three dead geese and his precious rifle. They agreed that when the Inupiat man returned to Barrow, Pinkham would take him before the district court judge. Pinkham trusted the man to turn himself in, as honesty is a core Inupiat value, yet Pinkham also knew that the arrest would not be popular in Barrow.

Pinkham paid a visit to Judge Sadie Neakok to explain what had happened. Neakok was Alaska's first native woman judge. She had been given the assignment in Barrow shortly after Alaska had become a state. She and the other native judges were trying to introduce U.S. justice in villages that preferred their traditional ways. Her "office" was her kitchen, and a bookshelf, entirely dedicated to law books, was under her husband's gun rack. As with most mothers, Neakok was a great multi-tasker. She conducted her official meeting with Pinkham while tending to her latest baby, her eleventh child.

Pinkham explained the Migratory Bird Treaty to Neakok, and offered her a deal. If she upheld the law while he was in Barrow, he would not mind if people shot ducks and geese while he was out of town. Neakok was shocked. Her people had been living off the land for centuries, so how could they be criminals? Rather than make a deal, she wanted the law changed.

On May 29, Pinkham walked down a Barrow dirt street with Johnny Nusunginya, a representative in the Alaska legislature. Nusunginya was carrying a rifle, as Barrow men often do. As the men walked, Pinkham explained the Migratory Bird Treaty and why he was enforcing it. He thought Nusunginya could be a perfect example to the locals if Pinkham could convince him to obey the law. While they talked, a flock of ducks flew by, and Nusunginya lifted his gun and shot one. It dropped to the ground. Nusunginya was pleased since his family now had dinner. He was completely surprised when Pinkham arrested him on the spot and took away his rifle.

As news of the arrest spread, the village was alarmed and knew they needed to act quickly. Sadie Neakok and Eben Hopson, Barrow's state senator, led a village meeting. Together they came up with a plan.

On May 30, Harry Pinkham received visitors at his office asking him to come outside. Pinkham opened his door to an amazing sight. Nearly the entire population of Barrow stood in the street, and everyone was holding a dead duck!

Baffled, he walked down to Neakok's house to ask her what to do. Neakok was sipping tea and looking out the window. She had been expecting him. After hearing him out, Neakok reminded him that he was required to fill out a form on every lawbreaker. Follow the law to the letter! Pinkham sighed, as it was not what he wanted to hear.

When Pinkham returned to his office, he found the 300-plus people signing a letter to President John Kennedy. The letter demanded that the president let the Barrow Inupiats hunt ducks and geese. The letter was given to Pinkham to deliver. Pinkham was learning the hard way how to be a public servant.

Pinkham sat at his desk and handwrote 138 notes. Each said that the person named had illegally shot a duck out-of-season. The Barrow residents proudly signed the notes, certifying their status as lawbreakers. While this was happening, Eben Hobson left briefly to send a telegraph to Governor William Egan, requesting that a social worker be sent to Barrow. The village's parents were going to jail and their children would be hungry. Barrow had no jail, so an old theater was opened to serve the purpose. It was a happy group of 138 prisoners who were housed in the "jail" that night.

Once Pinkham had dealt with the lawbreakers, he had to deal with the ducks. He had about ten large sacks of dead ducks, proof of the crime. Not owning an ice cellar large enough, Pinkham asked Sadie Neakok if he could store them in her cellar, but she refused. She wanted the government to see how difficult it was to enforce this law. Her family of thirteen lived off of the land. In fact, Sadie's husband was one of the jailed hunters.

It took Pinkham two small-plane flights to deliver all of the ducks to the Fairbanks office. He also submitted the letter to President Kennedy. He dreaded having to escort all 138 prisoners to Fairbanks, as that would take many more trips. Fortunately for Pinkham, the governor did not want that to happen either. In Juneau, Governor Egan called a special session of the Alaska legislature to discuss the crisis. They agreed to give Barrow natives permission to hunt duck and geese anytime. The 138 prisoners could go home to their families. Barrow had won!

The event was later referred to as the Barrow Duck-In. It forced all of Alaska, as well as the federal government, to consider the needs and traditions of Native Alaskans. Across Alaska, people applauded the Barrow Duck-In. If Barrow villagers could hunt ducks out-of-season, other natives reasoned that they could also. Alaska's Inupiat, Yupik, Aleut, Alutiiq, Eyak, Athabaskan, Tlingit, Tsimshian, and Haida people realized they had much in common. They knew that there were new challenges under statehood, but there were also new ways to voice their concerns.

The Barrow Duck-In inspired other native rights efforts in Alaska, and the shared purpose that had united Barrow drew natives across the state together over the issue of land ownership. They resented the fact that the federal government claimed ownership of all Alaskan land that it had not sold or awarded to others. In 1966, a native coalition demanded the return of their traditional lands. Their efforts brought about the Native Claims Settlement Act of 1971, which awarded large masses of land, plus financial compensation, to newly formed native corporations.

The federal government met with Mexico and Canada to mod-ify the Protective Migratory Bird Treaty, permitting arctic subsistence hunting. The Alaska Migratory Bird Co-Management Council, comprised of subsistence hunters and agency representatives, was created in 2003 to speak to the U.S. Department of the Interior.

Today, Barrow boys still follow their fathers to the marshland each spring to hunt ducks and geese. As the father watches over, the son carefully aims his rifle, shoots, and kills the bird. The father smiles, knowing that the family will enjoy duck soup that night, and that a new generation is learning traditional subsistence hunting skills.

THE MOLLY HOOTCH CASE

- 1972 -

Emmonak

MOLLY HOOTCH SIGNED HER NAME ON THE PETITION requesting a high school in her village of Emmonak. A fifteen-year-old Yupik Eskimo girl with a sweet smile, Molly dreaded leaving home in the coming fall of 1972 to travel to a faraway school.

At the time, Emmonak was a Yupik village of about 400, located near the mouth of the Yukon River. The village's Bureau of Indian Affairs (BIA) school only went through the eighth grade. Since Emmonak was off the Alaskan road-system, high school students could not be bussed to other schools or even commute during the week. Instead, these teenagers left home for a period of nine months. Each fall, parents lined the Emmonak airstrip to wave a teary good-bye to their sons and daughters.

During the school year of 1971–1972, Molly attended ninth grade in the city of Anchorage, which was over 500 miles away. She boarded with an Anchorage family who treated her like a servant and expected her to do much of the babysitting and housework. On the school bus, she was teased for wearing a Yupik fur parka and for being shy. In addition, the Anchorage school was larger than her whole village. Classes started and stopped at the ring of a bell, and people were always looking at clocks and watches. Molly missed the pattern of village life, which revolved around the seasons rather than clocks. She also missed the comfort of native foods, including seal oil and dried salmon. Like Molly, many other native children suffered terribly from homesickness when they were away at school. Telephoning home was almost impossible, as most villages had only one phone. Some teens found it easier to get into trouble in the larger communities, especially when it came to finding alcohol.

In addition to the problems the children faced, their families were affected by the gap they left behind. Villages were left with very few teenagers, and the chores traditionally done by them had to be assigned to other family members. Perhaps more importantly, traditional native skills were not being learned by the teens. In the end, many boarding school students quit and returned to their home villages feeling like failures. They brought back to the village poor habits learned at boarding school, including alcohol abuse.

There were twelve other Emmonak teenagers besides Molly who wanted a village high school. Village leaders knew that an in-town high school would help preserve family and community life, as well as the native language and culture. They also knew that they needed a lawyer to speak for them, and invited Chris Cooke from Alaska Legal Services to a village meeting. Cooke lived in the large Yupik community of Bethel on the Kuskokwim River. As requested, he flew to Emmonak and walked into the village hall to find it packed with people. Cooke was impressed by their energy and quickly decided that he would work to get them a high school. He handwrote notes as he talked to each of the thirteen teens, gathering their testimonials and using their own words to help make their case.

Cooke knew the task before him was a challenging one. He had petitions from fifteen teenagers in two other Yupik villages, Kwigillingok and Kongiganak, on Kuskokwim Bay. Both villages had BIA elementary schools, but no high schools. Together, the three villages had twenty-eight high school students. The distances between the communities mandated that each would need its own school.

Cooke needed to shape this information into a class-action lawsuit. One of the teens would have to be named in the title, and Cooke pondered which one it would be. He knew that the Alaska Commissioner of Education had taught in Emmonak's elementary school in the 1960s, and figured that he might remember some of the Emmonak children by name. That might help. Cooke studied the list of names for one that was short and catchy. Molly Hootch, the girl with the winning smile, was perfect! And thus, Molly's name represented the native children of high school age in 126 villages.

Cooke returned to his small Bethel office to begin work on *Molly Hootch vs. the Alaska State Operated School System.* He would tie the students' desire for local high schools to both the U.S. and Alaska constitutions. His argument was that native children needed the same school opportunities as white children, and the state had to realize that a K-12 education was every Alaskan child's right. He typed a paragraph describing each of the twenty-eight children, starting with Molly. Their situations described a stark reality. Eight of the teens had dropped out of school. One was in a BIA school in Sitka, 1,000 miles away. Six were in an Oregon BIA school, 2,100 miles away. Cooke pointed out that, in addition to the hardships this placed upon the students, their families, and villages, state taxpayers were paying the airfare and board for these children.

Cooke discovered that what was happening to these twenty-eight children and three villages fit into a troubling pattern. Prior to statehood in 1959, the territory provided schools for white children, while the BIA managed schools for native children. For decades, several communities had separate white and native schools. Yet in 1972, thirteen years after statehood, the federal BIA was still running most native schools.

Cooke dug up more information to expose the systematic discrimination in Alaskan schools. In 1972 one-third of Alaska's children had no local high school. Over 95% of the children who left home to go to high school were natives, while white communities smaller than Emmonak received state-funded high schools when they asked for them. Furthermore, while state-run high schools taught academics, BIA high schools taught work skills.

While only twenty-eight children were listed in the lawsuit, Cooke knew that the impact of winning the case would have a far greater reach than in just the three villages he was representing. For example, more than 1,000 students attended BIA boarding schools in Bethel, Kodiak, and Nome. Each of the schools was a failure. Over 40% of the Bethel dorm students dropped out after one year. The state had spent a lot of money building these boarding schools, but they had followed the advice of a Virginia company rather than talking to native parents about the design of the program.

While Chris Cooke was readying the lawsuit, Molly turned sixteen and returned to Anchorage for tenth grade. She was in a different high school and different boarding home, and luckily she was happier with both. Cooke submitted his eighteen-page lawsuit on October 5, 1972. The lawsuit of *Molly Hootch vs. the Alaska State Operated School System* became known as the Molly Hootch Case. The villages were said to be seeking Molly Hootch schools. The sweet girl from Emmonak was becoming famous.

Molly finished tenth grade in Anchorage and returned to Emmonak in the summer of 1973. Her father, John Hootch, didn't want her to return to Anchorage for eleventh grade, as her mother had divorced him and left the village. Suddenly, Molly's education was over. She was needed to keep house and watch after her six younger brothers and sisters, while her father hunted and fished. In addition to childcare, Molly cooked and made the family's fur clothing by hand. She also found a paying job in the village store. Molly still wanted a diploma, so she studied hard and earned her GED.

The Alaska Legal Service fought for native schools for four years. While they battled, the state gave Emmonak a high school, hoping that that would end the suit. As Emmonak and Molly no longer needed a high school, the name of the student in the case was changed to a girl in another village. Yet when a settlement was reached in 1976, most Alaskans were still calling it the Molly Hootch Case. In the settlement, each of the remaining 125 villages could choose whether they wanted a local high school. Of those, 105 asked for and received high school programs, and ninety-two new high schools were built. Village parents were asked to help shape the new curriculum. In addition to basic academics, many schools added native languages and skills.

The first Emmonak high school yearbook was dedicated to Molly Hootch. Emmonak and many other remote Alaskan villages owed her a big debt.

THE PIPELINE'S PERMAFROST PUZZLE

- 1977 -

Prudhoe Bay

WHEN THE PRUDHOE BAY OIL FIELD WAS discovered in 1968, it was the largest oil field ever found in North America. The oil companies were thrilled, but weren't quite sure how they could ship the oil to market if the closest seaway was frozen eleven months out of the year.

Houston oil company engineers looked at the map of Alaska and determined that the closest year-round port was Valdez. Then they drew a line from Prudhoe Bay to Valdez and discovered that their route crossed three mountain ranges, thirty-four rivers, and 800 streams. An 800-mile pipe was needed to transport the oil to Valdez. In order to build a pipeline, the companies had to first buy or lease the land underneath it.

The company that was going to undertake this massive project was the Alyeska Pipeline Service Company. To make it easier for Alyeska to buy and lease land, the U.S. government signed the Alaska Native Claims Settlement Act. This legislation paid the natives for the land the government was using, let them keep large tracks of tribal homeland not on the proposed pipeline route, and set up native corporations to manage their money and land. The settlement bore almost no resemblance to the reservation system found in the American West and generally pleased Native Alaskans as being long overdue.

Oil pipelines had been built before, but not above the Arctic Circle. When pumped from the ground, crude oil could be as hot as 160 degrees Fahrenheit. All existing pipelines carried oil while it was still warm, but no one was sure if this would work in the Arctic. Furthermore, much of the pipeline's right-of-way was frozen year-round, in a condition called permafrost. Parts of the area experienced temperatures of sixty degrees below zero during the winter and sixty degrees above zero during the short summer. As the snow melted, pools and streams formed on the tundra moss, above the frozen ground. The project engineers learned that the ground became mushy when warmed and that a heavy, warm object like a pipe could sink inches or feet into thawed muck. These engineers studied daily satellite pictures showing the extremes of the Alaskan landscape and temperature. Three hundred and fifty soil samples were collected along the pipeline route, and permafrost was found along 85% of it. The situation was a major challenge at best, but added to the mix was the fact that they were designing for an earthquake zone.

Four Houston oil company engineers packed heavy arctic clothing and traveled to Prudhoe Bay to see the conditions first-hand. The Arctic was foreign to them, and they felt like astronauts walking on another planet. In short order, the engineers set up a field lab. A 1,000-foot length of 40-inch steel pipe and several short lengths of smaller pipe were buried in the frozen ground. The engineers kept checking for damage to the pipe and surrounding permafrost. They studied the pattern of winter freezing and summer thawing to see if it would damage the pipe, and compared pipes of different sizes and thicknesses to see which could best withstand the pressure of icy permafrost and ice wedges, swords of ice that cut into the permafrost here and there. It became clear that in areas with icy permafrost, they would have to build the pipe above ground.

The engineers gave serious thought to cooling the oil to 30 degrees before sending it down the pipeline. However, Prudhoe Bay would need a great number of tanks to store the oil while it cooled. In addition, because cold oil moves slowly, they would have to build twice as many pump stations along the pipeline to keep the flow moving. Also, because cold crude oil left a waxy coating on the inside of pipes, frequent cleaning would be required. Sending warm oil from the wells down the pipeline was making greater sense to the engineers. They would have to design an insulated pipe to hold the warm oil without heating the surrounding ground or air.

A second lab was set up in central Alaska, near Fairbanks, where a 600-foot aboveground pipeline was created as an experiment. The engineers tinkered with the pipe, supports, and valves to perfect the design, and compared different steels and insulations. Based on their findings, the engineers chose very fine-grained steel. They designed a 48-inch steel pipe that was actually a pipe within a pipe, with a layer of insulation in between. Warm oil could flow through the interior pipe without warming the exterior one and thawing the surrounding permafrost.

About 400 miles of pipe would be buried underground or under streams. Under-stream pipes required an outer coat of cement to keep them sunk to the bottom. All of the underground pipe would be enclosed in a sandwich of different size gravels: bedding, padding, fill, and fill crown. Tall, 18-inch, metal poles would support the 400 miles of aboveground pipe. The supports were to be spaced every 50 to 70 feet, and atop each one, there would be two cooling devices that looked like metal bug antennas to wick any warmth from the ground to the air. The pipe would sit high enough to allow wildlife to walk under it. At each support, the pipe would rest in a metal saddle. "Shoe slides" would permit it to move a few inches when the ground heaved during spring thaw or an earthquake. The supports would also be cross-braced. If built according to plan, the pipeline would be permafrost-friendly, earthquake-proof, and wildlife-compatible!

The engineers carefully designed every piece of the project. Buildings at Prudhoe Bay would sit on deep-set pilings that looked like cement stilts. There would be eight pump stations along the pipeline to keep the oil moving. In Valdez there would be a number of huge oil storage tanks, known collectively as a "tank farm." They also designed a Valdez harbor for large oil tanker ships.

After spending 1500 man-hours planning the pipeline system, the engineers believed it would work. The federal government approved the design and gave the Trans-Alaska Pipeline the green light. It was time to build. The cost did not matter—Alyeska was willing to pay as much as needed to finish the job. Construction companies were eager to sign on for the job, and as the news traveled across America, people rushed to Alaska for high-paying work. Texas accents and cowboy boots became common in Prudhoe Bay, Fairbanks, and Valdez.

Construction of the Trans-Alaska Pipeline happened at a fast pace. First, Alyeska built a year-round, 360-mile road, the Haul Road, from Fairbanks to Prudhoe Bay. Built in an amazing five months, it was the first Alaskan road above the Arctic Circle. To aid the pipeline effort, the State of Alaska built the first bridge over the Yukon River. Thirty Alyeska construction camps and seventeen airstrips were set up along the pipeline route. There was a contest between the five pipeline section teams to see who would be finished first. Speed became the top priority.

Fairbanks, near the pipeline midpoint, became the supply center. Overnight, quiet Fairbanks turned into a boomtown. The population leaped from 40,000 to 60,000. Materials and people poured into

Fairbanks by road, rail, and airplane to be sent north and south along the pipeline. Fairbanks businesses were forced to pay high wages to keep their workers. Alaska rose to have the highest per-person income in the nation, and Alaska's population increased from 300,000 to 400,000 during the pipeline construction years.

On June 20, 1977, Prudhoe Bay's Pump Station Number 1 turned on the tap and warm crude oil flowed down the pipeline. It traveled at only a mile per hour. Teams of men on foot followed the sound of the flow, to see if the cold pipe would crack. It traveled uphill over the Brooks Range, crossed the Yukon River near Fairbanks, and climbed the Alaska Range and Chugach Mountains, before flowing into Valdez six weeks later. The pipe had not cracked, and the engineers were extremely pleased, not to mention relieved.

That first week 300,000 barrels of oil a day were piped through. When they were sure that the pipe could take the pressure, the quantity was increased to 1.2 million barrels daily. Construction had taken a little over three years, employed over 28,000 people, and cost a whopping $7.7 billion.

Alyeska had met its deadline, but there was a lot of wasted material during pipeline construction. Many pipe joints had weak welds that had to be redone. Some people refused to believe Alyeska's claim that the environment was left unharmed, wondering how something that had been done so quickly could have been done with environmental care and caution.

The Trans-Alaska Pipeline is still operating today. By 2001 it had moved over 14 billion barrels, was supplying 17% of the crude oil used by the United States, was funding 80% of Alaska's state government, and employed 1,000 people. Children in Fairbanks elementary schools learn to draw cross-sections of the pipeline support system, and tourists photograph each other standing by the pipeline . . . with caribou in the background.

LIBBY'S IDITAROD VICTORY

- 1985 -

Iditarod

IN 1973, THE FIRST IDITAROD TRAIL SLED DOG RACE was set from Anchorage to Nome, with the town of Iditarod as the halfway point. The total distance was said to be 1,049 miles, in observance of Alaska's standing as the forty-ninth state. Neither of the two race routes, however, was exactly that length. Alaskans immediately loved the Last Great Race and followed it closely every March. However, it took the first woman champion, Libby Riddles, to bring the Iditarod to the world's attention.

In 1985, twenty-eight-year-old Libby Riddles had been mushing for ten years and had finished two Iditarods. The village of Teller, where she lived, had faith in her skills and were her staunch supporters. Most race-watchers, however, regarded Libby as the prettiest musher on the field, but not a likely winner. Even among the five women mushers, she was a long shot!

On March 2, 1985, an excited crowd packed the sidewalk along Anchorage's Forth Avenue. Traffic was blocked off for the start of the race. Every two minutes, another of the sixty-one Iditarod teams was arranged at the starting line.

When it was her turn, Libby and eight friends readied her team of dogs. She was bundled in a blue parka with a fur ruff, and a fur hat covered her long blonde hair. She and her friends strained to hold the team of fifteen dogs back. Like wolves, huskies are pack animals that love to run.

"Three, two, one . . . GO!"

Libby let up on her brake, jumped on the runners, and gripped the handlebar. She gave a shout and the dogs bolted down Forth Avenue.

Before long the sixty-one teams were struggling in unusually deep snow. Booties protected the dog's feet, but their coats were becoming clumped with the white stuff. The wind blew snow over the trail and the orange trail markers. A few miles into the race, Libby's steel brake snapped in half. She knew it was unfixable. As she frantically looked around, she saw a friend in the crowd of onlookers. Luckily, he had a sled in his truck and was happy to give her its brake. In short order, the brake was replaced, and she was mushing again.

Libby's first-day problems were not over, however. Later that day, she tied her sled to a tree and rested the dogs and herself. The dogs should have been feeling somewhat fatigued, but they were so eager to join the passing teams that they bolted when she freed the rope from the tree. Libby was dragged until she lost hold of the rope. She managed to jump up and run after her team, now out of view. Waving, she flagged down the next racer, Chuck Schaeffer, who kindly gave her a ride. They found Libby's dogs staked out and her sled placed carefully on its side as an added anchor. Apparently her dogs had caught up with the next racer, and in the "work together" spirit of the Iditarod, he had done this favor for her. Libby sighed with relief as she checked over her dogs and the sled: all were unharmed. She thanked Schaeffer and vowed to reward the unknown musher who had caught her runaways.

The weather conditions were so awful during the race that the judges did something they had never done before—they paused the race! For three days, fifty-eight mushers and their 508 dogs camped at Rainy Pass, roughly 200-plus miles from Anchorage. The mushers were restless and the noise caused by 508 confined dogs was enough to drive them insane. Unfortunately, nearly 200 miles later, at McGrath, the race was paused for two more days. The rest revived Libby's spirits. She chose to be among the first of the mushers to leave McGrath, and stayed in a key spot from then on.

Libby was the fourth to mush into the midpoint ghost town of Iditarod. Volunteers came out of the checkpoint station to cheer her arrival. The checker wrote the time next to her name and number. As at the twenty-three other checkpoints, he looked into her sled bag to verify that she had all of the required gear. The vet quizzed Libby about the dogs' health and examined each animal. It was in his power to make a musher drop dogs from the team, leaving them at the checkpoint. In the notebook, he wrote that Libby's dogs looked healthy.

That evening, Libby left Iditarod with two other mushers, all with their headlights on. After slogging through thick snow, they caught up with the leader. Under normal conditions, the dogs are able to pull the sled through thick snow. Sometimes, however, it is too much to ask of the dogs, and the musher has to take some of the burden off of them by packing down the trail with snowshoes. The four mushers, who felt like both competitors and companions, worked together into the night. When they were too tired to go on, they fed their dogs and napped in their sleds. Travel became swifter on the Yukon River, where strong winds blew the loose snow away. Eventually the teams held their own paces and lost sight of each other.

At one point, Libby fell asleep while gripping her handlebar, and a low branch smacked her in the face. She woke up still clinging to the moving sled, with blood streaming down her cheeks: Luckily, her nose was not broken and her headlight still worked. Recalling her broken brake and runaway sled, she called this her "unlucky luck" and it stayed with her through the rest of the race. Libby was the first musher into the Eagle Island checkpoint, which was about two-thirds of the way along. She was privately thrilled and intended to keep the lead!

Arriving first at Shaktoolik, a checkpoint village on Norton Sound, Libby was greeted by a fierce storm brewing on the horizon. Nome was over 200 miles away, on the other side of the sound. To continue across the ice trail on this particular evening was dangerous, as the weather was kicking up. Libby checked in and weighed her options. She still had fourteen strong dogs, and she knew that her team was familiar with coastal storms in Teller, her village on the other side of Nome. Libby put her faith in her dogs and decided to risk a "storm run."

As the second racer arrived in Shaktoolik, Libby mushed into the blinding north wind. Sensing that they were going home, the dogs pushed on. Libby's fur-ruffed hood was cinched tight. Through her goggles, everything looked white. The trail markers, spruce poles set in the ice, were almost covered with snowdrifts. After a few slow miles, Libby took a nap in the sled basket. Even though they were moving slowly, they had kept their lead! Libby chalked it up to her "unlucky luck."

She was first into the next five checkpoints. At one, she decided to leave a favorite lead dog behind, so she left a note for the small plane pilot: "Take Sister to Nome." Libby's spirits nearly bubbled over at the last checkpoint, called Safety, since it was a 22-mile dash to the finish, and she was still in first.

On March 20, a crowd of thousands gathered on Nome's Front Street to watch Libby's team speed under the Iditarod Arch. She had won, and she had made history! Her risky "storm run" had paid off. It had taken her an unusually long eighteen days and twenty minutes, but the conditions were so extreme that a third of the racers would not even finish that year. This was twice the time and twice the number of scratches as in a typical race.

While television cameras rolled, Libby hugged Dugan and Axel, her final lead dogs. The two dogs received the Golden Harness Award for great leadership. In addition to the $50,000 first-place prize, Libby received the Humanitarian Award for her great dog care. As teams crossed the finish line, Libby found and questioned the mushers until she finally located and thanked the musher, named Terry Adkins, who had rescued her runaway team on the first day. Libby was thrilled when Adkins received the Sportsmanship Award. Chuck Schaeffer, Libby's other Good Samaritan, had scratched before finishing the race, but was still a hero in Libby's mind.

Libby's victory was reported in American newspapers, glossy magazines, and on television. The Women's Sports Foundation named her Sportswoman of the Year and she received a phone call from President Reagan. After 1985, America and the world followed the Iditarod Trail Sled Dog Race every year. More than just a sport, the race is about the Alaskan lifestyle, history, geography, and weather. It prizes good dog care and acts of kindness and rewards both the best rookie and the last to finish. Libby competed in three more Iditarods, never placing higher than sixteenth place. It mattered little; she would always be a champion in the eyes of Alaskans!

OIL SPILL IN
PRINCE WILLIAM SOUND

-1989-

Valdez

THE CREW OF THE *Exxon Valdez* looked at each other in horror. They had all heard it, the sickening, ripping sound of a jagged reef tearing into the hull of their supertanker. Moments later, the ship was grounded on the rugged spine of Bligh Reef. It was Good Friday, March 24, 1989, and crude oil began gushing into the pristine waters of Prince William Sound.

The sound is a blue-green jewel cradled by mountains. Glaciers flow between steep mountains and carve fjords in the coastline. Islands appear in the mist. Everything feels fresh and new, even in winter. The silence of a gorgeous day may be broken, but usually only by the cry of an eagle or the splash of an iceberg as it calves from a tidewater glacier.

Valdez, a small city of 3,500, is home to a major commercial salmon fishery and a growing nature-tourism industry. Since its harbor doesn't close seasonally, Valdez is also the terminus of the 800-mile Trans-Alaska Pipeline. During the planning of the pipeline in the 1970s, many warned of potential oil spills. But in twelve years of operation, nearly 9,000 tanker-loads of Prudhoe Bay crude had been shipped to outside refineries without a major spill. The Alyeska Pipeline Service Company and the U.S. Coast Guard had become complacent. Community complaints concerning the alcohol consumption of tanker crews were not taken seriously, and spill prevention and response capabilities slipped. On that tragic day in March, there was no available emergency response vessel. The barge reserved for spill containment equipment had been in repair for two weeks.

On the evening before the disaster, the *Exxon Valdez* had left for California with over fifty-three million gallons of crude oil. This was the tanker's twenty-eighth voyage, and the nineteen crewmembers were all old hands. It was a beautiful night. There was no fog, the water was calm, and the moon was bright. A pilot boat escorted the tanker through Valdez Narrows, as required, then returned to port. The tanker's captain, Joseph Hazelwood, radioed the U.S. Coast Guard for permission to temporarily leave the shipping lane to avoid an iceberg. Permission was granted for this common request, and since everything seemed safe and routine, Captain Hazelwood handed the wheel to his third mate, Gregory Cousins. Cousins was instructed to steer past tiny Busby Island and then head the tanker back into the southbound shipping lane. Hazelwood, along with his first and second mates, retreated to their quarters to sleep off the rest of the night, not expecting to rise until they were out of the sound.

Cousins would have viewed the responsibility as an honor, but he suspected that Captain Hazelwood had had a few drinks in Valdez before boarding the boat. Whether nervous or tired, Cousins mis-judged how many minutes ticked by. The tanker was well past Busby

Island when the lookout, Maureen Jones, warned him that they were heading into the shallow waters between Bligh Island and Bligh Reef. Cousins's heart sank and he panicked. He desperately tried to force the ship into deep water, but he misjudged the speed of the ship. The next sound he heard was the hull ripping over jagged Bligh Reef. Eight of the eleven cargo tanks were torn open. The impact violently shook the ship and woke all who were sleeping. It was four minutes after midnight.

A worried Hazelwood entered the wheelhouse. This was a tanker captain's worst nightmare. The crew knew they would be rescued, but they were also keenly aware of the impending damage to their careers. It was a full twenty-three minutes before Hazelwood found the nerve to radio the Coast Guard to report that they were "hard aground" and "leaking some oil." The captain's words were garbled, either from alcohol or stress, but the Coast Guard was not yet suspicious or alarmed. They sent a tugboat and two pilot boats, figuring that this was all the incident would require. A river of oil was already pouring from the tanker, but the Coast Guard had no clue that cleanup equipment was urgently needed.

Nearly three hours later, the *Exxon Valdez* radioed in that an estimated 5.8 million gallons of crude had been lost. Captain Hazelwood was finally telling the full truth, and the Coast Guard started to understand the magnitude of the problem. However, Alyeska's one cleanup barge was in repair, so another barge had to be found and stocked. Tragically, it was more than fifteen hours before it arrived at the scene with the emergency equipment, oil containment boom, and skimmers. A containment boom is a string of floats with dangling plastic strips meant to circle an oil slick, just as a swimming area is cordoned off at a beach. Done properly, the oil stays within this floating corral. However, so much time had been lost, that when the boom arrived, the slick had spread too wide. An empty, but smaller, tanker pulled beside the *Exxon Valdez* and oil was transferred to it. However, after it was full, there were still over forty-two million gallons inside the leaking supertanker.

Governor Steve Cowper flew over the entire spill area, which covered thirty-two square miles at that time. He was horrified by the slow and inadequate response. The president of the Exxon Shipping Company arrived from Houston, promising that Exxon would take full financial responsibility for the accident.

For the next two days, the water was calm. Yet, Exxon's experiments with chemical dispersants and burning proceeded slowly. "Too slowly," fretted the locals, who feared a turn in the weather. They were right to worry. On the third night the winds raged, blowing the enormous oil slick west toward the largest islands and beyond Prince William Sound, into the Gulf of Alaska. The howling winds churned the oil into a foamy goop the press called "chocolate mousse." By the fourth day the thickening black mess covered 500 square miles.

The people of Prince William Sound lost patience with Exxon's cleanup efforts. A cry went out to protect the sound's five salmon hatcheries. Several local fishing boats, nicknamed the "Mosquito Fleet," rushed to stretch boom at the mouth of the hatchery streams. The locals weren't the only ones alarmed by what they saw. Governor Cowper declared a state of emergency. He decided that the State of Alaska would conduct its own cleanup and bill Exxon; surely they could move more quickly than Exxon was. The Alaska ferry *E.L. Bartlett* went to work hauling boom to the most critical stops and housing cleanup crews. Despite their best efforts, the slick spread into the harbor of the island-village Chenega, washing over their shellfish and seaweed beds. Across the sound, people sprang into action. At the Chugach National Forest office in Anchorage, archaeologists, biologists, and soil scientists set protection priorities. They had to determine which beaches to shield, knowing that they lacked time and equipment to save every bird rookery and native village ruins. The slick spread out of Prince William Sound and headed west toward the city of Seward and two national parks. Seward was prepared to see the black goop spread into its harbor, but the fickle wind shifted, pushing the slick onto the shore of a national park instead. Seward residents jumped into action and helped the National Park Service clean beaches in two parks.

Reporters, volunteers, and people eager for high-paying jobs poured into Valdez. The pulse of Valdez quickened overnight. Six hundred flights a day arrived at the tiny airport, hotels filled up immediately, and residents rented out spare bedrooms. Some people slept on boats and in vehicles, while many others went without sleep, getting by on caffeine and hope.

A lot of that hope was poured into bird rescue centers. In addition to the birds, sea otters and sea birds were hosed and scrubbed. Sadly, few animals lived to be released back into the wild. Hours of film were shot, and the plight of these poor animals was documented for television audiences around the world. Many environmentalists made gloomy predictions of the fate of soon-to-return migratory birds, whales, seals, and fish. Foresters warned that bears and wolves would feast on oiled carcasses and die.

Exxon felt the sting of criticism and sped up their cleanup efforts, spending a tremendous amount of money in the process. On the beaches, teams suited in raingear scrubbed rocks and bagged debris. The slick continued to flow with the current, traveling some 460 miles. About 1,300 miles of shoreline were impacted. The damaged tanker was eased off of Bligh Reef in early April, a couple of weeks after it had become stuck. Approximately eleven million gallons, one-fifth of the tanker load, had been spilled. Cleanup continued through the summer and fall of 1989, and was conducted for three more summers before it was called off. Exxon claims that it spent about $2.1 billion on the cleanup, but evidence of oil is still found on some beaches today.

Luckily, the worst predictions did not come true. Prince William Sound does have a commercial fishery again, and no single species was lost entirely. However, an estimated quarter-million birds, 2,800 otters, 300 seals, 250 eagles, and 22 killer whales died. A total of twenty-seven species were identified as "injured." Ten years later the Harbor seal and Pacific herring, as well as six species of birds were still not showing signs of recovery. Alaskans, and the world, have learned how fragile the Great Land is.

Captain Hazelwood was convicted of negligence, as he was ultimately responsible for what happened on his ship. Exxon's criminal settlement exceeded the cost of cleanup. The money from this was used for numerous environmental restoration and research projects. Spill prevention and response capabilities are now of utmost importance, and oil tankers receive two-tugboat escorts through the entire sound. In Valdez oil companies are required to stock spill-response equipment adequate to contain, skim, and store oil from any future spills.

SMOKE AND FIRE

- 2004 -

Fairbanks

THE TEN BOATERS STOOD ON THE SANDBAR AND madly waved shirts, trying to catch the attention of the overhead plane. They relaxed when the plane circled closer and tipped its wing. They understood that there was no place for a plane to land, but hoped that word would get back to Fairbanks about their crisis. In the meantime, they would sit and wait for a helicopter rescue. A fire burned to the north of them and another to the south. They feared continuing on the river, not knowing if they might float into the blaze.

In late June of 2004, the group had driven about 100 miles north of Fairbanks to Birch Creek, in the Steese National Conservation Area. They hadn't considered it unusual that the air was a little smoky, as interior Alaska's summer season is casually referred to as the "fire season." They were willing to endure a little smoke in order to enjoy the wonders of one of America's wild and scenic rivers. However, their pleasant wilderness float soon became a journey through

Hell. The smoke had increased to a sickening cloud, and they soon spied blazing treetops to their north and south. On June 29, 40 miles down the creek, they pulled ashore, fearful of proceeding farther.

The frightened boaters spent two nights on the sandbar, hoping for an air rescue. When none came, they decided to float the creek. They had about 80 miles to paddle before reaching their vehicle, which was parked at the take-out point on the Steese Highway. If they pushed hard, they might be off the creek in three days. The guidebook warned them of Class III rapids 10 miles around the bend, but no one could predict if a blaze would jump the creek in the next few days. With bandanas over their noses and mouths, they put their boats into the water and pushed off. They were soon past the rapids and the creeks became gentle, but they could hardly admire the view. They gulped breaths of air and leaned into their paddles; the sky was so smoky that day looked like night. It might have been the Fourth of July when they reached the Steese Highway take-out. It was too early to celebrate, though, as they were still 100 miles out on the highway in the midst of a fire. They loaded what they could into the vehicles and crowded in, then drove south, trying to stay on the road while driving almost blindly through thick smoke. It was some time before they met a traffic manager. They asked him about the state of the fire. What they were told was worse than they had feared.

The fire had started on June 13 when a bolt of lightning streaked through the sky and struck a black spruce tree. The water-starved tree sparked and burst into flames. The fire quickly jumped to other trees, spreading along the dry moss and through the root system. Eventually, the plume of smoke was spotted over 50 miles away in Fairbanks. The fire was named the Boundary Fire.

This was different from other fire seasons, because the Alaskan interior was in the middle of the warmest summer on record. Everything was dangerously dry. Summer storms crackled with thunder and lightning, but dropped little rain. In just two days, lightning had started forty-seven fires.

An imaginary line across the interior is all that separates the U.S. Bureau of Land Management (BLM) lands from Alaska Department of Natural Resources (DNR) lands. The two agencies together watched as new fires exploded in the interior. Each blaze was given a name and mapped. Yet, the agencies both knew that firefighters rarely put out a wildfire, they merely tried to manage it. At first, BLM and DNR waited and watched.

Not long after the lightning storm came June 21, the summer solstice and longest day of the year. Alaskans loved to celebrate the day with picnics, but in 2004, the sky over the interior was gray and the air made eyes water. Softball games were canceled, since deep breathing was hazardous, and elderly people and children were told to stay indoors. Tourists left Fairbanks as quickly as they could to escape the smoke. Fairbanks residents stayed, with typical Alaskan resolve and humor, but they followed the news reports closely.

On June 24, lightning struck near a Fairbanks house, bumping power on the telephone line. The disturbance traveled down the line, and several hundred Fairbanks phones stopped working. Things looked even worse on June 26. Strong winds blew the flames southward and the Boundary Fire jumped the Steese Highway, between Fairbanks and Circle along the Yukon River. Immediately, the 160-mile highway was closed and Circle's residents were cut off. Traveling by car was out of the question, flying was dangerous, and boating down the Yukon River might take them through another fire area.

The 200 villagers of Venetie, on the Chandalar River, watched the smoky sky. The wind was blowing a raging fire toward them. Their only escape was by boat on the Chandalar River or by airplane, but no one wanted to leave their homes. As the fire came within 2 miles of the village, the BLM considered evacuating everyone.

The wind blew another fire toward the large Pogo Mine. When it was just 2 miles away, it appeared that the gold mine camp would be lost. Eighty miners, eager to go home, were flown to safety.

The BLM and DNR fire managers realized that they needed to work together and with the City of Fairbanks. Fairbanks doctors had never seen smoke this thick before and feared for the health of the people. The entire Alaska interior seemed to be ablaze. Forest fires elsewhere in the state were keeping the U.S. Forest Service and National Park Service busy. Alaska needed outside help. An urgent plea for firefighters was sent to the Lower Forty-Eight.

When the winds shifted on June 27, a few hundred Alaska firefighters jumped into action. They had three areas where they initially focused. The first crews were sent to the Steese Highway to beat the fire back to the north side of the road. Another crew went to Venetie, where a stroke of good luck shifted the winds and stopped blowing smoke into town. The evacuation of Venetie wasn't necessary, and villagers were allowed to stay. Everyone knew that the winds were fickle and could shift again, but people began to feel more hopeful as firefighters arrived with water pumps, and soon hoses pumped river water over Venetie homes and the surrounding tundra. The situation was also improving at the Pogo Mine, where the wind was now blowing the fire away from the mine. Some miners helped firefighters wet down the mine area and remove as much brush, the fire's fuel, as possible. They were battling, but not winning the war.

Overnight, winds whipped up the Boundary Fire, doubling it. When Fairbanks folks woke on June 30, the fire was just 30 miles away. The fire managers told everyone living north of Fairbanks to come south. Lodges, gold mines, and cabins were abandoned as hundreds fled to Fairbanks. The passengers of each escaping vehicle wondered if they were the last to drive down the Steese Highway. So far, only one cabin had been lost, but everyone feared that would change.

At the start of the Fourth of July weekend, more than two weeks after the fires had begun, the winds shifted again. Fires raged toward the Elliott, Taylor, and Dalton highways, and another fire jumped the Chena Hot Springs Road, cutting off the resort from Fairbanks.

When the sun peeked through the smoke on July 4, some in Fairbanks saw this as a hopeful sign. A new team of fire managers arrived that day to relieve the weary few in charge. On the morning of July 5, they met at the Fairbanks army base and made a plan of attack, aiming to focus their efforts on thirteen of the sixty-two fires.

Firefighters were brought up from forty-six states, to aid the 750 Alaska firefighters already in the field. At the height of the effort, there were over 2,700 people engaged in the firefight across Alaska. New firefighters soon learned that fighting fires in Alaska was different from in other states. The midnight sun permitted round-the-clock firefighting. Crews of sixteen people worked twenty-one-day shifts, which sometimes lasted sixteen hours a day. Crews were housed in remote lodges, mining camps, and tent camps. Each camp had at least one armed guard to protect the crew and kitchen from bears. Food was stored in a hole dug into the permafrost.

In a state with few roads, maintaining each road was vital. Many of the summer travelers were tourists, and rather than totally close interior roads, pilot cars led convoys of cars and RVs safely through walls of smoke as long as 100 miles. Fires began to subside on July 18, and late summer rains aided the larger firefighting crews in their battle. When the first snow dusted the mountaintops in August, the fire was over. The team had won the war!

The 2004 summer fire season was the worst in Alaska's history. The fires left a 5.5 million-acre scar in the Alaska interior, an area about the size of New Hampshire. Another million acres of burned land peppered the rest of Alaska. Fires had come alarmingly close to several communities, including Fairbanks, the second largest city in the state. Although it defies logic, no one had died or been seriously injured.

ALASKA FACTS & TRIVIA

* "Alaska" comes from a native word, Alyeska, meaning the "Great Land."

* Early man walked from Asia across the Bering Land Bridge to Alaska about 11,000 years ago.

* There are about 98,000 Alaska natives, and they make up about 16% of the state's population. These native people are the Athabaskan, Tlingit, Haida, Tsimshian, Alutiiq, Aleut, Yupik, and Inupiat. Under the 1971 Alaska Native Claims Settlement Act, twelve native regional corporations were created.

* Alaska is the largest state in the union, covering 570,374 square miles or about 365 million acres, making it one-fifth the size of the entire Lower Forty-Eight.

* Alaska has nearly 34,000 miles of shoreline. It borders the Pacific Ocean, Bering Sea, Chukchi Sea, and Arctic Ocean.

* Alaska has 1,800 named islands. The largest is Kodiak Island.

* Alaska shares a border with Canada, over 1,500 miles long. It is not connected with any of the states.

* The Arctic Circle passes through northern Alaska. Scientists know it as the place where the sun does not set on Summer Solstice (June 21), and does not rise on Winter Solstice (December 21).

* Alaska has approximately 100,000 glaciers, covering about 5% of the state. The largest is the Malaspina Glacier.

* Alaska has seventeen of the twenty tallest mountains in the United States. Mount McKinley (Denali), at 20,320 feet, is the tallest peak in North America.

* The Yukon River starts in Canada and flows across Alaska, cutting the state in half. Fourteen hundred of the river's 1,875 miles are in Alaska.

* North America's largest recorded earthquake was Alaska's Good Friday Earthquake on March 27, 1964.

* Alaska's Tongass National Forest and Chugach National Forest are the largest and second largest national forests in the country.

* The National Park Service has fifteen parks, preserves, and monuments in Alaska. The list includes Denali National Park and Preserve, Glacier Bay National Park and Preserve, Katmai National Park and Preserve, and Sitka National Historic Park.

* Alaska's capital is Juneau, which is located on the Alaska Panhandle. Many are surprised to discover that Juneau is connected to the rest of the state by ferry rather than road.

* The population of Alaska is under 650,000, making it the second least populated state in the union.

* The largest city in Alaska is Anchorage, with a population of over 260,000.

* Seward Day (March 27) celebrates the purchase of Alaska by the United States from Russia in 1867. Alaska Day (October 18) marks the day in 1867 that the American flag was first raised over Sitka, the former capital of Russian America.

* Alaska became the forty-ninth state in 1959.

* The Alaska flag has a blue background with a golden Big Dipper and North Star. The design, created by thirteen-year-old Benny Benson, was selected in 1927.

* Alaska's state song is called "Alaska's Flag."

* The "Alaska Bush" is any area not on the road system. Many Alaska villages can only be reached by plane, boat, or snow machine.

* Alaska has a state ferry system known as the Alaska Marine Highway. Nine ferries connect many communities that are not on the road system.

* The world's busiest seaplane base is Lake Hood in Anchorage, Alaska.

* Nearly all of Alaska is in one time zone, Alaska Standard Time.

* The Iditarod Trail Sled Dog Race has been run every March since 1973. The race from Anchorage to Nome is close to 1,049 miles long.

* There are five kinds of salmon: king salmon (chinook), silver salmon (coho), red salmon (sockeye), pink salmon (humpie), and dog salmon (chum). The largest Alaska king salmon recorded weighed over ninety-seven pounds.

* A few crops thrive in the Land of the Midnight Sun, such as pumpkins, squash, and rutabagas. America's largest cabbage, weighing over 105 pounds, grew in Alaska.

* The Alaska Pipeline runs from Prudhoe Bay to Valdez, a distance of about 800 miles.

* The Exxon Valdez Oil Spill in Prince William Sound took place on Good Friday, March 24, 1989.

* California naturalist John Muir made three trips to Alaska. An 1880 visit to Glacier Bay inspired his book, *Stickeen.*

* California writer Jack London was in Alaska for the Klondike gold rush, 1897–1898. His Klondike experiences were the basis for his books *The Call of the Wild* and *White Fang.*

* In 1920, New York artist Rockwell Kent wrote *Wilderness: A Journal of Quiet Adventure in Alaska,* about his year on an Alaskan island.

* Alaska's state flower is the forget-me-not.

* Alaska's state gem is jade.

* The state mineral of Alaska is gold.

* Alaska's state tree is the Sitka spruce.

* The state bird of Alaska is the willow ptarmigan.

* The Alaska state fish is the king salmon.

* The state sport of Alaska is dog mushing.

* Alaska's nickname is "The Last Frontier."

* Alaska's motto is "North to the Future."

BIBLIOGRAPHY

General Sources

Alaska Atlas and Gazetteer: Topo Maps of the Entire State. Freeport, Maine: DeLorme Mapping, 1992.

Gates, Nancy, ed. *The Alaska Almanac: Facts About Alaska,* 27th ed. Portland, Oregon: Alaska Northwest Books, 2003.

Russians Meet Alaskans on the Rocks!—1741

Hunt, William R. *Arctic Passage: The Turbulent History of the Land and People of the Bering Sea, 1679–1975.* New York: Charles Scribner's Sons, 1975.

Shalkop, Antoinette, ed. *Exploration in Alaska: Captain Cook Commemorative Lectures June–November 1978.* Anchorage: Cook Inlet Historical Society, 1980.

The Search for the Northwest Passage—1778

Hunt, William R. *Arctic Passage: The Turbulent History of the Land and People of the Bering Sea, 1679–1975.* New York: Charles Scribner's Sons, 1975.

Shalkop, Antoinette, ed. *Exploration in Alaska: Captain Cook Commemorative Lectures June–November 1978.* Anchorage: Cook Inlet Historical Society, 1980.

Slaves of the Seal Harvest—1786

Elliott, Henry W. *The Seal-Islands of Alaska*. 1881. Reprint, Kingston, Ontario: The Limestone Press, 1976.

Henning, Robert A., ed. "Island of the Seals: The Pribilofs," Alaska Geographic Society 9, no. 3, (1982) 1–123.

Hunt, William R. *Arctic Passage: The Turbulent History of the Land and People of the Bering Sea, 1679–1975*. New York: Charles Scribner's Sons, 1975.

The Battle of Sitka—1802 & 1804

Calvin, Jack. *Sitka: A Short History*. 1936. Reprint, Sitka: Old Harbor Press, 1983.

Flaherty, Thomas H. Jr., ed. *The Alaskans*. Virginia: Time-Life Books, 1977.

National Park Service, National Parklands in Alaska (Anchorage, 2002).

Pierce, Richard A., ed. *Russia in North America: Proceedings of the Second International Conference on Russian America: Sitka, Alaska, August 19–22, 1987*. Kingston, Ontario: The Limestone Press, 1990.

Little Girl on a Bering Sea Whaler—1857

Garner, Stanton, ed. *The Captain's Best Mate: The Journal of Mary Chipman Lawrence on the Whaler Addison, 1856–1860*. Providence, R.I.: Brown University, 1966.

Hunt, William R. *Arctic Passage: The Turbulent History of the Land and People of the Bering Sea, 1679–1975.* New York: Charles Scribner's Sons, 1975.

Rebel Raiders in the Bering Sea—1865

Hunt, William R. *Arctic Passage: The Turbulent History of the Land and People of the Bering Sea, 1679–1975.* New York: Charles Scribner's Sons, 1975.

Naval Historical Center. www.history.navy.mil.

Science and Madness on the Yukon River—1865

Flaherty, Thomas H. Jr., ed. *The Alaskans.* Virginia: Time-Life Books, 1977.

Hunt, William R. *Arctic Passage: The Turbulent History of the Land and People of the Bering Sea, 1679–1975.* New York: Charles Scribner's Sons, 1975.

Sherwood, Morgan B. *Exploration of Alaska: 1865–1900.* New Haven, Connecticut: Yale University Press, 1965.

Webb, Melody. *Yukon: The Last Frontier.* Lincoln, Nebraska: University of Nebraska Press, 1993.

Did America Buy Fort Yukon?—1869

Flaherty, Thomas H. Jr., ed. *The Alaskans.* Virginia: Time-Life Books, 1977.

Hunt, William R. *Arctic Passage: The Turbulent History of the Land and People of the Bering Sea, 1679–1975.* New York: Charles Scribner's Sons, 1975.

Sherwood, Morgan B. *Exploration of Alaska: 1865–1900.* New Haven, Connecticut: Yale University Press, 1965.

Webb, Melody. *Yukon: The Last Frontier.* Lincoln, Nebraska: University of Nebraska Press, 1993.

Adventure on Ice—1880

Muir, John. *Stickeen: The Story of a Dog.* 1909. Reprint, Garden City, N.Y.: Doubleday and Company, 1974.

Sherwood, Morgan B. *Exploration of Alaska: 1865–1900.* New Haven, Connecticut: Yale University Press, 1965.

Young, S. Hall. *Alaska Days with John Muir.* New York: Fleming H. Revell Company, 1915.

Cook Inlet Shipwreck—1890

Allen, Lois. *Alaska's Kenai Peninsula: The Road We've Traveled.* 1946. Reprint, Hope, Alaska: Kenai Peninsula Historical Society, 2002.

Cook, Linda and Frank Norris. *A Stern and Rock-Bound Coast: Kenai Fjords National Park Historic Resource Study.* Seattle: Government Printing Office, 1998.

Shipwrecks Off Alaska's Coast. www.mms.gov/alaska/ref/ships.

Powerful Giving—1890

Bancroft-Hunt, Norman and Werner Forman. *People of the Totem: The Indians of the Pacific Northwest.* London: Orbis Publishing Limited, 1979.

Cooper, Doreen C. *A Century at the Moore/Kirmse House.* Skagway, Alaska: Klondike Gold Rush National Historical Park, 2001.

Moore, J. Bernard. *Skagway in Days Primeval.* New York: Vantage Press, 1968.

Reindeer Rescue—1894

Antonson, Joan M. and William S. Hanable. *Alaska's Heritage.* Anchorage: Alaska Historical Commission, 1985.

Baiki: The International Sami Journal. www.baiki.org.

Flaherty, Thomas H. Jr., ed. *The Alaskans.* Virginia: Time-Life Books, 1977.

Hunt, William R. *Arctic Passage: The Turbulent History of the Land and People of the Bering Sea, 1679–1975.* New York: Charles Scribner's Sons, 1975.

Rennick, Penny, ed. "Alaska's Seward Peninsula," Alaska Geographic Society 14, no. 3 (1987) 1–109.

Death on the Glacier—1897

Barry, Mary J. *A History of Mining on the Kenai Peninsula, Alaska.* Anchorage: MJP Barry, 1997.

Avalanche on the Chilkoot Trail—1898

Canadian Parks Service, *A Hiker's Guide to the Chilkoot Trail* (Whitehorse, 1991).

Davis, Mary L. *Sourdough Gold: The Log of a Yukon Adventure.* Boston: W.A. Wilde Company, 1933.

Pennington, Gerald L. *Klondike Stampeders Register: A Chronology of the Klondike Gold Rush, 1897–1898.* Skagway: Pennington, 1997.

Soapy Smith Shot in Skagway—1898

Pennington, Gerald L. *Klondike Stampeders Register: A Chronology of the Klondike Gold Rush, 1897–1898.* Skagway: Pennington, 1997.

Harriman Bags His Bear—1899

Antonson, Joan M. and William S. Hanable. *Alaska's Heritage.* Anchorage: Alaska Historical Commission, 1985.

Hott, Lawrence et al. *The Harriman Alaska Expedition Retraced 1899-2001.* VHS. Florentine Films/Hott Productions, Incorporated, 2002.

Lord, Nancy. *Green Alaska: The Far Coast.* Washington, D.C.: Counterpoint, 1999.

Railroad Wars—1907

Alaska's Virtual Library and Digital Archives. http://vilda.alaska.edu.

Hunt, William R. *Distant Justice: Policing the Alaska Frontier.* Norman, Oklahoma: University of Oklahoma Press, 1987.

Valdez Museum and Historical Archive. www.valdezmuseum.org.

Mount Katmai Erupts—1912

Barry, Mary J. *A History of Mining on the Kenai Peninsula, Alaska.* Anchorage: MJP Barry, 1997.

Clemen, Janet and Frank Norris. *Building in an Ashen Land: Historic Resource Survey of Katmai National Park and Preserve.* Anchorage: National Park Service, 1999.

Freeman, Nancy, ed. "Kodiak: Island of Change," Alaska Geographic 14, no. 3 (1977) 1–96.

National Park Service, "Witness: Firsthand Accounts of the Largest Volcanic Eruption in the Twentieth Century" (Anchorage, 2004).

To the Top of Denali—1913

Moore, Terris. *Mt. McKinley: The Pioneer Climbs.* College, Alaska: University of Alaska Press, 1967.

Rennick, Penny, ed. "Denali," Alaska Geographic 15, no. 3 (1988) 1–90.

Saving Nome—1925

Iditarod Trail Sled Dog Race: Official Site of the Last Great Race. www.iditarod.com.

Rennick, Penny, ed. "Alaska's Seward Peninsula," Alaska Geographic 14, no. 3 (1987) 1–109.

Salisbury, Gay and Laney Salisbury, "Endurance, Fidelity, Intelligence: The 1925 Serum Run Made Heroes of Alaska Sled Dogs," Alaska. March 2005.

Welcome Back, Musk Ox—1930

Alaska Department of Fish and Game. www.adfg.state.ak.us.

Couch, Jim. "Those Imported Musk Oxen," in *The Alaska Book: Story of Our Northern Treasureland.* Chicago: J. G. Ferguson Publishing Company, 1960.

Sparks, Kathy. *Song of the Muskox.* Unionville, Ind.: The Hand Maiden, 1993.

University of Alaska, Fairbanks: History of UAF. www.uaf.edu/uaf.

Japanese Capture Kiska Island—1942

Garfield, Brian. *The Thousand-Mile War: World War II in Alaska and the Aleutians.* Fairbanks: University of Alaska Press, 1995.

Rennick, Penny, ed. "World War II in Alaska," Alaska Geographic Society 22, no. 4 (1995) 1–80.

Barrow Duck-In—1961

Blackman, Margaret B. *Sadie Bower Neakok: An Inupiaq Woman.* Seattle: University of Washington Press, 1989.

Gallagher, Hugh Gregory. *Etok: A Story of Eskimo Power.* 1974. Reprint, Clearwater, Florida: Vandamere Press, 2001.

The Molly Hootch Case—1972

Alaskool. www.alaskool.org.

Molly Hootch vs. Alaska, 72 AK 2450 (1972).

The Pipeline's Permafrost Puzzle—1977

Allen, Lawrence J. *The Trans Alaska Pipeline: The Beginning,* vol. 1. Seattle: Scribe Publishing Corporation, 1975.

Hanrahan, John and Peter Gruenstein. *Lost Frontier: The Marketing of Alaska.* New York: W. W. Norton and Company, Inc., 1977.

Roscow, James P. *800 Miles to Valdez: The Building of the Alaska Pipeline.* Englewood Cliffs, N.J.: Prentice-Hall, Inc., 1977.

Libby's Iditarod Victory—1985

Iditarod Trail Sled Dog Race: Official Site of the Last Great Race. www.iditarod.com.

"Libbymania Helped Propel Race," *Anchorage Daily News,* 15 June 2005.

Mattson, Sue, ed. *Iditarod Fact Book: A Complete Guide to the Last Great Race.* Kenmore, Wash.: Epicenter Press, 2000.

Riddles, Libby and Tim Jones. *Race Across Alaska: First Woman to Win the Iditarod Tells Her Story.* Harrisburg, Penn.: Stackpole Books, 1988.

Oil Spill in Prince William Sound—1989

Exxon Valdez Oil Spill, 1989. www.u-s-history.com/pages/h2405.html.

Exxon Valdez Oil Spill Trustee Council. www.evostc.state.ak.us.

O'Donoghue, Brian. *Black Tides: The Alaska Oil Spill.* Anchorage: Alaska Natural History Association, 1989.

Smoke and Fire—2004

Bohman, Amanda and Beth Ipsen. "Hundreds Evacuate as Fires Move In," *Fairbanks Daily News-Miner,* 1 July 2004.

Braun, Curt. *Alaska Wildland Fires 2004.* Tucson, Ariz.: Wildland Fire Lessons Learned Center, 2004.

Ipsen, Beth, "New Team Takes Over Boundary Fire," *Fairbanks Daily News-Miner,* 5 July 2004.

Jettmar, Karen. *The Alaska River Guide.* Anchorage: Alaska Northwest Books, 1993.

Joling, Dan, "Forest Fire Burn on Half-Million Acres of Alaska Forest," *Anchorage Daily News,* 29 June 2004.

Mowry, Tim, "Heavy Smoke Strands Group on Birch Creek," *Fairbanks Daily News-Miner,* 1 July 2004.

Smetzer, Mary Beth, "Lightning Cause of Dead Phones," *Fairbanks Daily News-Miner,* 2 July 2004.

INDEX

ABOUT THE AUTHOR

Diane Olthuis moved to Alaska in 1977 to teach on remote St. Paul Island. She has hiked the Chilkoot Trail, climbed Denali, canoed the Yukon River, and kayaked Glacier Bay. The tiny community of Hope is her home. Diane is the author of Historic Building Survey Report: *Hope, Alaska and Goldpan* and *Trapline & Camera: The Harry A. Johnson Album.*

We have Alaska covered

Death in the Grizzly Maze
THE TIMOTHY TREADWELL STORY

INSIDERS' GUIDE
The Kid's Guide
CRUISING ALASKA
Eileen Ogintz
with Reggie Yemma

INSIDERS' GUIDE
Off the Beaten Path
FIFTH EDITION
alaska
A GUIDE TO UNIQUE PLACES
MELISSA DeVAUGHN

"A tender chronicle of a miracle in process . . ." —Kirkus Reviews
the ONLY KAYAK
KIM HEACOX
A Journey into the Heart of Alaska

INSIDERS' GUIDE
SCENIC DRIVING
ALASKA AND THE YUKON
Second Edition
ERIK MOLVAR

Whether you're looking for the path less traveled, a favorite place to eat, family-friendly fun, a breathtaking hike, enchanting local attractions, or a good read, our books are filled with ideas to help you get the most out of your time in Alaska or enjoy an armchair adventure there.

The Globe Pequot Press
FALCON GUIDE
INSIDERS' GUIDE
LP LYONS PRESS

For a complete listing of all our titles, please visit our Web site at www.GlobePequot.com.
Available wherever books are sold.